To Pastor Donald Barsuhn, whose faithful ministry
has enriched every church he has served

PREACH
FOR A
YEAR #6

104 Sermon Outlines
Two complete outlines for every Sunday of the year

Roger Campbell

Kregel
Academic & Professional

Preach for a Year #6 by Roger F. Campbell

Copyright © 2002 by Kregel Publications, a division of Kregel, Inc., P.O. Box 2607, Grand Rapids, MI 49501. Kregel Publications provides trusted, biblical publications for Christian growth and service. Your comments and suggestions are valued.

For more information about Kregel Publications, visit our web site at: www.kregel.com.

Scripture quotations are from the King James Version of the Holy Bible.

ISBN 0-8254-2329-5 (vol. 1)
ISBN 0-8254-2330-9 (vol. 2)
ISBN 0-8254-2321-x (vol. 3)
ISBN 0-8254-2318-x (vol. 4)
ISBN 0-8254-2347-3 (vol. 5)
ISBN 0-8254-2386-4 (vol. 6)

1 2 3 4 5 / 06 05 04 03 02

Printed in the United States of America

CONTENTS

CONTENTS

INTRODUCTION

What is preaching?

It is teaching, but it is more than teaching.

Paul preached with passion, sometimes with tears. And if God is to increase the effectiveness of our preaching, we must do the same.

John Wesley was once asked by a young preacher how he could get more people to attend his church. Wesley answered, "Get on fire and people will come to watch you burn."

John Bunyan wrote, "I preached what I did feel, what I smartingly did feel."

Luther said, "I preach as if Christ was crucified yesterday, rose from the dead today, and is coming back to earth again tomorrow."

Preaching thus needs a depth of both passion and faith. And preachers often need, too, a little practical help. The response to the first five books in my "Preach for a Year" series has encouraged me to write number six. Letters and phone calls have come from near and far, telling me how God has used these topical-expository outlines to help busy pastors feed their sheep and reach lost people for Christ. *Preach for a Year #6* contains outlines that will enable pastors to provide their hearers with the spiritual nutrition needed for growth, maturity, and outreach.

The effectiveness of this book, however, will be the results of pastors, servants of God, who refuse to allow these outlines to be merely organized information. These preachers will invest prayer and passion in their delivery and, therefore, make them their own.

All quotes of Spurgeon are from my book *Spurgeon's Daily Treasures in the Psalms* (Nashville: Nelson, 1997).

The final section of this book contains four sermons suitable for "preacher occasions," such as installations, ordinations, and so forth. Exhorters sometimes need exhorting too.

ROGER CAMPBELL

No Fear This Year

Genesis 15:1

I. Introduction

A. *Fear Will Spoil the New Year for Many*
 1. Fear is common to all, the first evidence of the Fall (Gen. 3:10)
 2. Fear robs life of adventure and joy, bringing gloom instead of gladness

B. *Note the First "Fear Not" in the Bible*
 1. It was given to Abram, the man of faith
 2. Fear and faith are opposites; as faith increases, fear decreases
 3. Sometimes, like Abram, we experience fear after a great victory

C. *A Promise Was Given to Abram to Overcome His Fears*

II. Body

A. *Note the Person Making This Promise*
 1. A promise is only as good as the person making it
 2. This promise is from the Lord
  a. He is the One who made heaven and earth (Ps. 121:2)
  b. He is the One who cannot lie (Titus 1:2)
  c. He is the One who can do anything but fail (Jer. 32:17; Luke 1:37)
 3. We can stand securely on the promises of God
  a. God's promises will hold when trouble comes
  b. Let the promises of God drive your fears away
 4. Every problem we'll face this year is covered by the promises of God
 5. We can enter the year with confidence in our unfailing God

B. *Note the Protection Accompanying This Promise*
 1. "I am thy shield"
 2. Moses told Israel they had been saved by the Lord, their shield (Deut. 33:29)

3. David called the Lord his shield
   a. "Our help and our shield" (Ps. 33:20)
   b. "The LORD God is a sun and shield" (Ps. 84:11)
4. "The Christian still finds light and shelter in the Lord his God, a sun for happy days and a shield for dangerous ones" (Spurgeon)
5. Faith in God shields us from Satan's attacks (Eph. 6:16)
6. Solomon said God is a shield to those who trust in Him (Prov. 30:5)

C. *Note the Prospects Resulting from This Promise*
1. "I am thy . . . exceeding great reward"
2. Abram had refused the rewards of the king of Sodom
   a. Abram with 318 servants had rescued Lot and others from Chedorlaomer (chap. 14)
   b. He could have had great rewards for this rescue but turned them down
   c. Could he now have been having second thoughts about this?
3. The Lord would be a greater reward to him than anything he could have received
4. Do you see the Lord as your reward, more valuable than all earthly gains?

III. Conclusion

A. *God Meets Us Where We Are, Offering Salvation (John 6:37)*
B. *God's Promise of Peace Is to All Who Come to Jesus (Matt. 11:28–30)*
C. *God's Protection Is Given to Those Who Belong to Him (Isa. 41:10)*
D. *The Lord Himself Is the Reward of Those Who Believe (Gen. 15:1)*

No Faith, No Future

Genesis 15:1–6

I. Introduction
A. *The Call of Abram Had Been Accompanied by Promises*
1. He was promised a new land (Gen. 12:1)
2. He was promised that he would have many descendants and be a blessing (v. 2)
3. He was promised protection from enemies for him and his family (v. 3)

B. *Abram Stepped Out on Faith in God's Promises*
1. He departed and began his great adventure of faith
2. Have you begun the life of faith by taking Christ as your Savior?
3. Have you entrusted your future to Him?

C. *The Future Belongs to Those Who Place Their Faith in Jesus*

II. Body
A. *Note How Faith Affects Our Family (vv. 1–3)*
1. The call of Abram had to do with families (Gen. 12:1–3)
   a. Abram was to leave for Canaan with his family
   b. He was to be a blessing to all families of the earth
2. God is interested in our families
   a. Noah and his family were called into the safety of the ark (Gen. 7:1)
   b. The Philippian jailer was offered salvation for him and his family (Acts 16:31)
3. Abram struggled with unbelief over having a family (Gen. 15:3)
4. God promised him a seed; Paul said this blessed seed was Christ (Gal. 3:16)
5. Our faith in Christ should be examples to our families

B. *Note How Faith Affects Our Future (vv. 4–5)*
1. What if Abram had not dared embark on his adventure of faith?
   a. There would have been no promised blessings for him and his family

15

        b.   He would have missed out on life's greatest adventure

    2.   Faith assured his future

        a.   He would be led to the Promised Land

        b.   He would have descendants who would be a blessing

        c.   His name would be great and remembered . . . and it is

    3.   Consider the scope of these blessings (vv. 4–5)

        a.   He would have a son in his old age

        b.   His descendants would be as the number of stars

C. *Note How Faith Affects Our Fellowship with God (v. 6)*

    1.   Faith brought Abram into a right relationship with God

        a.   He believed God, and it was counted to him for righteousness

        b.   Abram, a sinner, was justified before God by faith

    2.   What good news this is for you and me!

        a.   We are all sinners (Rom. 3:10–23)

        b.   Christ died to save sinners (Rom. 3:25; 5:8)

        c.   Like Abram, we are justified by faith (Rom. 4:1–5)

III.   Conclusion

A. *Are You an Example of Faith to Your Family?*

B. *Does Faith Make You Confident About Your Future?*

C. *Do You Have Fellowship with God Through Faith in Christ?*

Kept Alive for Life's Greatest Adventure

Joshua 14:10–15

I. **Introduction**
   A. *Caleb Was the Optimistic Spy*
      1. Caleb was sent to scout the Promised Land
      2. He was one of twelve spies sent by Moses (Num. 13:6)
      3. Caleb returned, believing Israel could conquer Canaan (Num. 13:30)
   B. *Caleb Was the Spy Who Outlived the Doubters*
      1. All the spies died except Caleb and Joshua
      2. Faith and positive action are life extenders
   C. *Caleb Became a Senior on His Greatest Adventure*

II. **Body**
   A. *Caleb Had Been Kept Alive for This Adventure (v. 10)*
      1. "The LORD hath kept me alive"
      2. We have been kept alive for the adventures of this new year
      3. God has a lifelong purpose for each of us
      4. Advancing years add to the adventure
         a. Caleb now had more wisdom than when younger
         b. Caleb had gained more respect from his family and friends
         c. Caleb's faith had increased with age
         d. Caleb was better able to serve than ever before
      5. Too many shrink from adventures in faith because of their age
      6. Don't let advancing years keep you from life's greatest adventures
   B. *Caleb Had Strength for This Adventure*
      1. At eighty-five, he refused to believe he was too weak to succeed
         a. He focused on strength rather than weakness
         b. Some older people think only of their ailments
         c. Caleb at eighty-five thought of the joy of adventure

17

    2. Caleb viewed his strength as sufficient for whatever was ahead

       a. He said he was as strong at eighty-five as at forty-five

       b. He was strong enough to travel into Canaan

       c. He was strong enough to go to war expecting victory

    3. Christ provides strength for the day (Deut. 33:25; Phil. 4:13)

C. *Caleb Believed God Had Equipped Him for This Adventure*

    1. "Give me this mountain"

    2. God has equipped us for what He wants us to do

    3. Age brings new adventures

       a. Travel may take us on adventures in new places

       b. Health problems may bring us into contact with needy people

       c. Wisdom will enable us to be better servants of God

       d. Understanding will give us greater compassion for hurting ones

III.   Conclusion

A. *Doing God's Will Is Life's Greatest Adventure*

    1. The adventure begins with salvation by grace (Eph. 2:8–9)

    2. God has great adventures planned for all who believe

B. *Have You Surrendered for Life's Greatest Adventure?*

God Calling

1 Corinthians 1:26–31

I. **Introduction**
   A. *God Calls People*
       1. He called Adam and Eve after the Fall
       2. He called Noah in a violent age
       3. He calls people today
   B. *God Calls People to Salvation (Matt. 11:28–30)*
   C. *God Calls People to Service (Rom. 1:1)*
   D. *Who Does God Call?*

II. **Body**
   A. *God Calls the Foolish (v. 27)*
       1. He called foolish Zacchaeus
           a. Zacchaeus had lived only for what he could accumulate
           b. His main goal in life was to become wealthy
           c. He had cheated others to get ahead
           d. He was called down from a sycamore tree to be saved
               (1) Zacchaeus was short, and we've all fallen short
               (2) "He was a come shorter" (Ironside; see Rom. 3:23)
       2. God called foolish Jonah, who tried to run away from Him
           a. Many are still trying to run away from God
           b. How foolish to think we can escape God's call
       3. He called the foolish to wisdom and eternal life
   B. *God Calls the Weak (v. 27)*
       1. He called the prodigal son
           a. The young man was so weak, he was out of control
           b. He was so weak, he squandered his inheritance
           c. He was so weak, he gave in to bad company
       2. God has called weak people to do mighty things
           a. D. L. Moody was untrained but brought many to Christ

19

        b.   Mel Trotter was a drunkard but then mighty for God
    3.   Why does God use nobodies?
        a.   It shows His power to change lives
        b.   Thus, people will see the miracle and turn to Christ

C.   *God Calls the Base and the Despised (v. 28)*
    1.   He called the woman at the well to reach her town
        a.   She had been married five times and was now living with one not her husband
        b.   Christ gave her living water and quenched her spiritual thirst
        c.   She brought others to find the Savior
    2.   He called harlots and lepers, to the amazement of the Pharisees
    3.   He's still calling outcasts to salvation because of His love

III.   Conclusion
A.   *Have You Thought You Were Out of the Reach of God's Love?*
B.   *Have You Thought Your Sins Were Too Serious to Be Forgiven?*
C.   *God Is Calling You to Salvation and Service*
D.   *Will You Respond to His Loving Call?*

A Miracle with a Message

Acts 3:1–12

I.   Introduction
   A. *Note the First Miracle After Pentecost*
       1. The call of Christ came at Pentecost (Acts 1:4–8)
       2. The great revival began at Pentecost (Acts 2)
           a. The Holy Spirit came at Pentecost (Acts 2:1–4)
           b. The apostles witnessed in a language understood by all (Acts 2:4–6)
           c. At Peter's sermon, three thousand were saved (Acts 2:41)
   B. *It Was More than a Miracle*
       1. The healing of the lame man was a miracle with a message
       2. "Notice how the miracle and message coincided" (Ironside)
       3. What is the message of this miracle?

II. Body
   A. *Two Went to the Temple to Pray (v. 1)*
       1. The temple was different than before the Cross
           a. The veil had been torn in two (Matt. 27:51)
           b. All can come into the Holy of Holies through faith in Christ
       2. Peter and John came to pray at the ninth hour
           a. It was the traditional hour of prayer at the temple
           b. It was the time when the evening sacrifices were made
           c. It was a time to announce Christ's sacrifice to pay for our sins
       3. Prayer makes miracles possible and our message powerful
   B. *One Went to the Temple to Plead (vv. 2–3)*
       1. He was lame in his feet
           a. Had been lame from birth
           b. We all walk lamely because we are sinners (Rom. 3:10–23)

2. He had been living on the world's handouts
    a. All sinners seek something to satisfy their emptiness
    b. The handouts of the world leave us beggars still
3. This lame man needed something the world couldn't give

C. *One Went into the Temple with Praise (vv. 4–8)*
    1. Peter saw the beggar's real need and met it
    2. The beggar expected a gift of money
        a. Peter said, "Silver and gold have I none"
        b. Peter had a greater gift to be given: "Such as I have give I thee"
    3. The miracle: "In the name of Jesus . . . rise up and walk"
        a. Peter took him by the hand and lifted him up
        b. With the gospel message we can lift others from sin and shame
    4. The man, now healed, began to leap and praise God

III.   Conclusion

A. *Note the Reaction of Others to the Miracle (vv. 8–11)*
    1. The people were amazed
    2. The miracle created an opportunity to preach the gospel
B. *We Ought to Seize Opportunities to Tell Others of Christ*
C. *Salvation Is the Greatest Miracle of All*

Shaking Off the Vipers

Acts 28:1–6

I. Introduction
- A. *Follow Paul on His Journey to Rome*
    1. Paul was going to Rome as a prisoner
    2. Many trials awaited him in Rome
- B. *Recall the Storm and the Shipwreck*
    1. Paul was comforted by an angel in the storm (Acts 27:22–25)
    2. They were shipwrecked and stranded on an island, but all alive
    3. They were met by kind natives, a warm fire, and trouble ahead
- C. *A Viper, Coming Out of the Fire, Attacks Paul*
    1. Vipers often appear out of the fires of life
        a. Times of trouble make us vulnerable
        b. God has a promise for the fiery times (Isa. 43:2)
    2. Paul shook off the viper when attacked, and so should we

II. Body
- A. *Shake Off the Viper of Discouragement (v. 3)*
    1. Paul was attacked while helping . . . doing good
        a. He was gathering a bundle of sticks for the fire
        b. Vipers often appear when we're doing right
    2. Paul could have allowed this attack to make him doubt
    3. Instead, he shook off the viper, remembering God's promise of safety
    4. Let God's promises deliver you; shake off discouragement
- B. *Shake Off the Viper of Criticism (v. 4)*
    1. The reaction of the critics: "No doubt this man is a murderer"
    2. Many are quick to judge and falsely accuse
        a. Are you being wrongly judged, falsely accused?

      b.   You are not the first to endure this kind of trial

   3.   Jesus was constantly criticized

      a.   He was called a blasphemer (Matt. 9:3)

      c.   He was accused of being in league with Satan (Matt. 9:34)

   4.   Remember how Jesus responded to His critics (1 Peter 2:23)

   5.   Shake off the viper of criticism by looking to Jesus (Heb. 12:1–2)

C. *Shake Off the Viper of Low Expectations (v. 6)*

   1.   The natives expected Paul to swell up and die

   2.   Some have low expectations of you as a Christian

      a.   They think you'll stumble and fall

      b.   They're waiting for you to backslide

   3.   Shake off the faithless conclusions of others

   4.   Prove them wrong by being faithful to your Lord

III. Conclusion

A. *Jesus Came to Give Us Abundant Life (John 10:10)*

   1.   We can have daily victory in spite of the opposition

   2.   The Holy Spirit has equipped us to win

B. *Shake Off Those Vipers and Experience the Joy of the Lord*

Christch and Communion

I. Introduction

   A. The Hour of the Ages Approaches
      1. "My time is at hand" (26:18)
      2. The Crucifixion nears (26:2)

   B. Jesus Prepared the Disciples for the Coming Cross
      1. They shared the last Passover (the types to be fulfilled at the Cross)
      2. They shared the first Communion (a new covenant begins)

   C. Note These Lessons from Jesus for Every Communion Service

II. Body

   A. Remember the Communion and Christ's Body (v. 26)
      1. "Take, eat; this is my body"
      2. The disciples must have wondered about that statement
         a. Christ was in His body
         b. The disciples could see His body
      3. Luke clears up the mystery (Luke 22:19)
         a. "In remembrance of me"
         b. The bread is to be a symbol to remind us of Christ's body
      4. What should we remember about His body at Communion?
         a. Christ chose the limitations of a body (Phil. 2:5–7)
         b. Christ chose to show His love in a body (Phil. 2:8)
      5. Christ endured the pain of the Cross in His body

   B. Remember the Communion and Christ's Blood (vv. 27–28)
      1. "He took the cup, and gave thanks, and gave it to them"
      2. "Drink ye all of it; For this is my blood"
      3. How could this be Christ's blood?
         a. The disciples knew His blood was in Him

         b.   Like the bread, this was a memorial, a symbol of His blood

         c.   This was clear to the disciples and should be to us

    4.   Christ's blood was shed to pay for our sins (Rom. 5:9)

         a.   Christ's blood has redeemed us (1 Peter 1:18–19)

         b.   Christ's blood cleanses us from sin (1 John 1:9)

         c.   Christ's blood proves His love for us (Rev. 1:5)

    5.   Remembering His blood at Communion should increase our love for Him

   C.   *Remember the Communion and Christ's Coming Kingdom (v. 29)*

    1.   "In my Father's kingdom"

    2.   Communion looks in two directions

         a.   It looks back to the Cross

         b.   It looks forward to the kingdom

    3.   Communion is a time to search our hearts and confess our sins

    4.   It is a time to celebrate our wonderful future with Christ in His kingdom

III.   Conclusion

   A.   *When We Remember the Cross, We Become Aware of Our Sins*

   B.   *Have You Responded to the Love That Makes Forgiveness Possible?*

   C.   *Will You Be with Christ in His Wonderful Kingdom?*

Christat After Communion

Matthew 26:26–42

I. **Introduction**
  A. *Witness the First Communion*
    1. Christians everywhere break bread and share the cup of Communion
    2. Communion began with Jesus and His disciples around a table
  B. *The First Communion Was a Preview of the Cross*
    1. It was a preview for them; it is a memorial for us
    2. It is a time to remember the Savior's death and anticipate His return
  C. *What Pictures of Jesus Develop Following the First Communion?*

II. **Body**
  A. *Here Is a Picture of the Singing Savior (v. 30)*
    1. "When they had sung an hymn they went out"
    2. What kind of hymn did they sing?
      a. Jesus had given thanks for the bread and cup
      b. Their song was likely one of thanksgiving
    3. Christ, thankful during Communion, is a mystery of grace
      a. He was thankful for the coming Cross
      b. Thankful for spit? For spite? For spikes?
      c. He was thankful for salvation being available to all
    4. Every Communion service should give us a song of praise
      a. Christ paid for our sins with His blood
      b. This is the unending song of heaven (Rev. 5:9)
  B. *Here Is a Picture of the Sorrowing Savior (vv. 36–38)*
    1. "He began to be sorrowful"; "My soul is exceeding sorrowful"
    2. The closeness of the coming Cross breaks in on Jesus
      a. He recognizes the pain, the shame, the suffering ahead

27

         b.   He will fulfill Isaiah's prophecy of the
            suffering servant (Isa. 53)
     3.   Some will leave this service to face unknown
       sorrows
         a.   Most go through sorrows they didn't think
            they would
         b.   Many go through sorrows they didn't think
            they could
     4.   The sorrowing Savior understands and cares
     5.   "God is with us in sorrows. There is no pang that
       rends the heart. I might almost say, not one which
       disturbs the body, but what Jesus Christ has been
       with you in it all" (Spurgeon)

C.   *Here Is a Picture of the Submissive Savior (v. 42)*
     1.   "Thy will be done"
         a.   They are the four most difficult words to pray
         b.   These words mean submission to the Cross
     2.   This is the expression of a submissive heart in
       prayer
         a.   How long has it been since you uttered a
            prayer like this?
         b.   How long since your heart was truly submitted
            to God's will?

III.   **Conclusion**
     A.   *Will You Leave This Communion Table More Like*
         Jesus?
     B.   *Will You Leave with a Song Because of His Love for*
         You?
     C.   *What Picture of Christ Is Developing in You for Others*
         to See?

Why All This Groaning?

Romans 8:18–27

I. Introduction

A. *There Are Better Days Ahead*
   1. There are better days ahead for all creation
   2. There are better days ahead for all Christians

B. *Meanwhile, There's a Lot of Groaning Going On*
   1. Creation is groaning
   2. Christians are groaning
   3. The Holy Spirit is groaning

C. *What's All This Groaning About?*

II. Body

A. *Why Is Creation Groaning? (vv. 18–22)*
   1. "The whole creation groaneth" (v. 22)
      a. This was not the case in the beginning
      b. Everything God made was good (Gen. 1:31)
   2. The Fall brought pain to the whole creation (Gen. 3)
      a. It brought sickness, sorrow, and death to mankind
      b. It brought thorns, thistles, storms, and earthquakes to the world
      c. It brought enmity among and between animals and humans
   3. This groaning of nature reminds us of the seriousness of sin
   4. Like a woman in travail, creation awaits Christ's return
   5. An increase in natural disasters is a sign of that great day (Matt. 24:7)

B. *Why Are Christians Groaning? (vv. 23–25)*
   1. "Not only they, but ourselves also" (v. 23)
   2. One would think believers would have nothing to groan about
      a. Our sins are forgiven through faith in Christ (Eph. 1:7)
      b. We are justified and have peace with God (Rom. 5:1)
      c. We are assured of a home in heaven (John 14:1–3)

    3. Why, then, do we groan?
        a. We are part of a fallen, sinful, race (Rom. 3:10–23)
        b. We experience pain, suffering, and death like others (Heb. 9:27)
    4. We groan because we know a better day is coming (Rom. 8:18)
        a. We groan in anticipation of the coming resurrection
        b. At adoption (son-placing) day, our bodies will be perfect

  C. Why Is the Holy Spirit Groaning? (vv. 26–27)
    1. The Holy Spirit helps our poor praying
        a. We groaning ones don't know how to pray as we ought
        b. The Holy Spirit intercedes for us with groanings that cannot be uttered
    2. The Holy Spirit knows what is best for us and intercedes accordingly
    3. Trouble is God's call to prayer; the Comforter makes our praying effective

III. Conclusion

  A. Glory Follows Groaning for Creation and Christians
  B. Creation Waits the Day When Men and Angels Say, "Behold, the Savior Comes Again!"
  C. That Day Is Getting Closer All the Time

Knowing God

Exodus 33:13–14, 17

I. Introduction
   A. *Why Should Anyone Want to Know God?*
      1. No God . . . no peace (Isa. 57:21)
      2. Know God . . . know peace (John 14:27)
      3. Something is missing in life until we know Him
   B. *Knowing God Is the Heart's Greatest Desire*
      1. Knowing God surpassed every other desire of
          Moses
      2. What is the supreme desire of your heart?
   C. *How Can We Know God?*

II. Body
   A. *We Can Know God Through Faith in His Word (v. 13)*
      1. "If I have found grace in thy sight"
      2. There is no hope for anyone apart from God's
          grace
         a. Grace grants God's favor to undeserving
             sinners
         b. Only grace makes it possible for sinners to
             know God
      3. This grace is made personal and practical through
          faith
         a. Faith appropriates God's grace by believing
             His Word
         b. Paul said this enabled him to know God
             personally (2 Tim. 1:12)
      4. Moses had come to faith long ago (Heb. 11:23–29)
      5. Now he wanted to know God better
      6. Do you know God? How well do you know Him?
   B. *We Can Know God Through Focusing on His Way
       (v. 13)*
      1. "Shew me now thy way, that I may know thee"
      2. We know God better by observing His works
         a. We know Him by learning about His plan of
             creation and redemption
         b. We know Him by studying the work of God
             among His people

31

        c.   We know Him by comparing Old Testament prophecies and New Testament fulfillment

    3.   Studying the life of Jesus helps us know God better
        a.   We get a greater appreciation of His love
        b.   We get a better understanding of His grace

    4.   Lingering at the Cross draws us closer to God

    5.   Focusing on Christ's return makes us more like Him (1 John 3:1–3)

C. *We Can Know God Through Full Surrender to Him (v. 14)*

    1.   "My presence shall go with thee"

    2.   Moses had been called to a difficult task
        a.   He had undergone many trials
        b.   God had been with him all the way

    3.   God's faithfulness in trials moved Moses to want to know Him better

    4.   He was willing to keep following wherever God's will led him

III. Conclusion

A. *Do You Long to Know God?*

B. *Do You Long to Know Him Better?*

        a.   Trust Christ as your Savior and know Him personally

        b.   Study His Word and His way . . . and surrender fully to Him

The Power of a Forgiving Church

Acts 1:14; Matthew 18:15–17;
Mark 11:25; Ephesians 4:30–32

I. Introduction
  A. *Look at a United Church*
   1. They were all of one accord (Acts 1:14)
   2. They were praying together in one place (Acts 2:1)
   3. They were of one heart and soul (Acts 4:32)
  B. *This Church Had Many Potential Problems*
   1. Peter had denied Christ three times
   2. Thomas had doubted the Resurrection
   3. The women had gone to the tomb to do the work of undertakers
   4. Love enabled them to forgive and shake the world (Acts 17:6)
  C. *There Are Three Bible Calls to Forgiveness*

II. Body
  A. *Forgive to Restore a Brother (Matt. 18:15–17)*
   1. It is a simple straightforward plan
   2. Your brother has sinned against you
     a. You go to him alone, not telling anyone else
     b. You go immediately, praying for reconciliation
   3. You lovingly tell your brother what divides you
   4. If he responds, you forgive him and are reconciled to him
   5. If he does not respond, you go to the church in an effort to gain your brother
  B. *Forgive So That Your Prayers Are Not Hindered (Mark 11:25)*
   1. "And when you stand praying, forgive"
   2. Effective prayer is vital to any church
     a. The first meeting of the early church was a prayer meeting
     b. When believers agree in prayer, good things happen
   3. We cannot pray effectively unless we forgive
   4. "It is obvious that every Christian who tries to pray with unforgiveness in his heart finds a great wall

33

of his sins piled up between him and God which he cannot get removed and cannot get taken out of the way until he forgives all that others have done against him" (John R. Rice, *Prayer: Asking and Receiving* [Murfreesboro, Tenn.: Sword of the Lord, 1942], 295).

    5.   Lack of forgiveness may keep your prayers from being answered

C. *Forgive So You Do Not Grieve the Holy Spirit (Eph. 4:30–32)*

    1.   Why did the early church have such great power?

       a.   The members were weak and imperfect people

       b.   The Holy Spirit was the source of their power

       c.   They were filled with the Holy Spirit

    2.   When we do not forgive, we grieve the Holy Spirit

       a.   When we stop grieving the Holy Spirit, His power flows through us

       b.   Spirit-filled people are not in bondage to malice and anger

    3.   We can forgive because we have been forgiven (v. 32)

III. Conclusion

A. *Who Awaits Your Forgiveness?*

B. *Go to That Waiting One and You Will Not Go Alone*

Let's Plug into the Power

Acts 4:31–33

I. Introduction
- A. *We Are All in Need of God's Power*
    1. We need His power to live the Christian life
    2. We need His power to overcome the enemy of our souls
    3. We need His power to reach a lost world
- B. *All the Power We Need Is Available to Us*
    1. We have the promise of power in the Great Commission (Matt. 28:18–20)
    2. Paul longed for the power of the Resurrection (Phil. 3:10)
    3. The early church had power to change the world (Acts 17:6)
- C. *How Can God's Great Power Be Ours?*

II. Body
- A. *We Must Plug into the Power of Prayer (v. 31)*
    1. "And when they had prayed"
        - a. The place was shaken
        - b. They were all filled with the Holy Spirit
    2. The message is clear: *power comes through prayer*
    3. The disciples asked the Lord to teach them to pray (Luke 11:1)
        - a. We are well taught in many things: organization, doctrine, teaching techniques
        - b. Too many are illiterates in the school of prayer
        - c. We learn to pray by asking big and expecting answers
    4. Prayer brings the power of the Holy Spirit
    5. Prayer brings boldness in telling others of Christ
- B. *We Must Plug into the Power of Love (v. 32)*
    1. "[They] were of one heart and of one soul"
    2. Christian fellowship in a church is built on love
    3. All Christian effort is useless without love (1 Cor. 13)
        - a. Love forgives and breaks down barriers

35

    b. Love looks for the best in our brothers and sisters

    c. Love is considerate of others in the church

   4. Love produces a passion for lost ones in the community

   5. Love enables Christians to put away their differences

   6. Love makes people more important than possessions

 C. *We Must Plug into the Power of Witnessing (v. 33)*

   1. "With great power gave the apostles witness"

    a. These praying, loving people became powerful witnesses

    b. They witnessed of the power of the Cross and Resurrection

   2. Evangelism is the greatest need of our time

   3. Churches languish because so few witness for Christ

   4. Witnessing Christians are a powerful force for God

III. Conclusion

 A. *Consider the Accomplishments of the Early Church*

   1. Without our advantages, they put us to shame

   2. They stressed the basics and won thousands to the Lord

 B. *We Must Get Back to the Basics of Christianity*

 C. *Prayer, Love, and Witnessing Will Shake the World for Christ*

New Beginnings

2 Corinthians 5:17–20

I. **Introduction**
   A. *The Christian Life Has a Beginning*
      1. No one is born a Christian; all are born sinners (Ps. 51:5; Rom. 3:10–23)
      2. All need to be born again to receive eternal life (John 3:1–5, 16)
   B. *Sometimes Even Believers Need New Beginnings*
      1. We need a new beginning when we become bitter or bothered about the past, present, or future
      2. David understood this and prayed for a new beginning (Ps. 51)
   C. *Follow the Simple Steps to a Believer's New Beginning*

II. **Body**
   A. *Let the Past Be Past Through Forgiveness (v. 17)*
      1. "Old things are passed away"
         a. Let's believe this regarding our past sins (Ps. 103:12)
         b. Let's believe it regarding confessed sins since salvation (1 John 1:9)
      2. Refuse to be tormented by sins God has forgiven
      3. New beginnings also require forgiving others (Eph. 4:30–32)
         a. Many are held back in their Christian walk by refusing to forgive
         b. It is time to put away old grudges for wrongs done to us
      4. We can forgive because we have been forgiven
         a. We have never been wronged like we have wronged God
         b. Since He has forgiven us, we can forgive others
      5. Are you ready to let the past be past through forgiveness?
   B. *Let the Future Be Fantastic Through Faith (v. 18)*
      1. "All things are of God"

    2. We begin with God by faith at salvation (Rom.
5:1; Eph. 2:8–9)

    3. The entire Christian life is an experience in faith

       a. The just shall live by faith (Hab. 2:3; Rom.
1:17; Gal. 3:11; Heb. 10:38)

       b. Faith is total trust in the Lord; it is the opposite
of fear

       c. As faith increases, fear decreases

    4. Why then are so many believers in bondage to
anxieties?

       a. They are not trusting God for everyday
provisions (Phil. 4:19)

       b. They are trying to face the future before it
arrives (Matt. 6:34)

       c. They have forgotten all things are possible
with God (Luke 1:37)

    5. "Faith makes the uplook good, the outlook bright,
the inlook favorable, and the future glorious"
(V. Raymond Edman)

C. *Let the Present Be Exciting Through Evangelism
(vv. 18–20)*

    1. "God . . . hath given to us the ministry of
reconciliation"

    2. We have been commissioned to tell others of
Christ's love

       a. We are ambassadors for Christ

       b. We are to bring others to be reconciled to God

    3. Nothing is as exciting as winning others to the
Savior

III. Conclusion

A. *Have You Begun with Christ? Are You Born Again?*

B. *Have You Lost the Joy of Your Salvation?*

C. *Let Forgiveness, Faith, and Evangelism Bring You a
New Beginning*

What's So Important About the Rapture?

1 Corinthians 15:51–52; Revelation 22:12

I. Introduction

A. *Jesus, Who Died and Rose Again, Will Come Again*
1. His death, burial, and resurrection offer eternal life
2. These are the ingredients of the gospel (15:3–4)
3. His return will fulfill His promise (John 14:1–3)
4. His return for His church is called "the Rapture"

B. *Why Is Focusing on the Rapture So Important?*
1. Many focus on the time of the Rapture (signs, etc.)
2. Many focus on the details of the Tribulation, which follows the Rapture
3. We need a new focus on the Rapture itself
4. Why is this true?

II. Body

A. *The Rapture Will Bring Resurrection (1 Cor. 15:51–52)*
1. Read Paul's great chapter on the Resurrection (chap. 15)
    a. Here is the importance of the resurrection of Christ (15:12–20)
    b. Here is the importance of the resurrection of believers (15:20–23)
    c. The Resurrection is our comfort when we lose loved ones (1 Thess. 4:18)
2. The Resurrection will take place at the Rapture
3. The dead in Christ will rise first (15:52)
4. Every visit to a cemetery should remind us of the coming Rapture
5. Have you experienced the comfort found in the promise of resurrection at the Rapture?

B. *The Rapture Will Bring Recovery (1 Cor. 15:51–52)*
1. "We shall be changed"
2. Living believers will be caught up in a moment
    a. That magnetic moment will change us all
    b. We will be like Jesus (1 John 3:1–2)
3. We will recover what Adam and Eve lost
    a. We will have perfect bodies unhindered by pain

        b.   We will have perfect minds no longer affected by the Fall

        c.   We will have no more sickness, sorrow, or death

    4.   All creation awaits what will be revealed on that wonderful day (Rom. 8:18–23)

        a.   Creation still groans because of the Fall

        b.   Then creation will glory in what God has done for His people

C.   *The Rapture Will Bring Rewards (Rev. 22:12)*

    1.   Christ will come bringing rewards with Him

    2.   Rewards for what?

        a.   Faithful service for our Lord will be rewarded

        b.   Overcoming temptation and steadfastness in trials will be rewarded (James 1:12)

        c.   Looking for and loving our Lord's appearing will be rewarded (2 Tim. 4:8)

    3.   Let's live in anticipation of that coming day

III. Conclusion

A.   *Are You Ready for the Rapture?*

B.   *Have You Trusted Christ as Savior?*

C.   *What Rewards Await You When Your Lord Returns?*

Caught Away

1 Thessalonians 4:13–18

I. Introduction
A. *What Is the Next Great Prophetic Event?*
1. Many prophecies were fulfilled in the birth of Jesus
2. Many prophecies were fulfilled in Christ's death and resurrection
3. The next great prophetic event is Christ's return

B. *What Will Happen When Christ Returns?*
1. The dead in Christ will be raised (vv. 13–16)
2. Living believers will be caught away (v. 17)

C. *Three Questions Are Raised by the Imminency of Christ's Return*

II. Body
A. *How Shall We Live in Light of the Countdown?*
1. Each day brings us closer to Christ's return
a. The prophetic clock never stops
b. Time's relentless march brings an urgency to life
2. The countdown of life keeps reminding us of the shortness of time
a. Dreams realized or dashed keep us aware of the importance of seizing opportunities
b. The absence of those now in heaven alerts us to the brevity of life
3. The countdown to Christ's return is made evident by signs all about us
a. One sign is wars and rumors of war (Matt. 24:6–7)
b. Another sign is new diseases and natural disasters (Matt. 24:7)
c. Another sign is the days of Noah: increased iniquity in an affluent time (Matt. 24:37–39)

B. *How Shall We Live in Light of the Catching Away?*
1. "We which are alive and remain shall be caught up" (v. 17)
2. The One who died and rose again will come again

41

    3. Believers alive at that time will escape death
       a. Death has taken its toll through the centuries
       b. We've all stood by the graves of loved ones
       c. A better day is coming—the day we'll be caught away
    4. Our plans then ought to transcend our brief stay on earth
       a. Laying up treasures here should not have priority
       b. We ought to live every day with Christ's coming in mind (1 John 2:28)

Expectancy

  C. *How Shall We Live in Light of the Coming Judgment?*
    1. The judgment seat of Christ follows the Rapture
       a. We must all appear before the judgment seat of Christ (2 Cor. 5:10)
       b. Christians must give an account of their service for Christ (Rom. 14:12)
    2. Examination day is on its way
    3. Rewards await those who have served Christ faithfully
    4. Peter challenges us all: Everything we see will perish (2 Peter 3:11)
    5. How will our Lord judge your service for Him?

III. Conclusion
  A. *Does Your Future Hold Rewards or Regret?*
  B. *There Is Still Time to Surrender Your Life to Christ*
  C. *You Can Begin to Lay Up Rewards Today*
  D. *Don't Delay! You May Soon Be Caught Away!*

Joy in Trials?

James 1:1–12

I. Introduction

   A. James Writes to the Family of God: "My Brethren"

      1. We become part of God's family through faith (Rom. 5:1)

      2. You can become a child of God by receiving Christ (John 1:12)

   B. James Also Writes About Joys and Trials

      1. We are to see trials as joy

      2. How can this be?

         a. Trials are not joyful

         b. How can we be joyful in them?

II. Body

   A. We Can Look Past Our Trials (vv. 2–4)

      1. "The trying of your faith worketh patience"

         a. Patience looks forward to better things

         b. Patience looks beyond today's clouds to sunshine

      2. Jesus has set the example at the Cross (Heb. 12:2)

         a. The pain and shame of the Cross made it a terrible trial

         b. Jesus looked beyond these to the joy that would follow

      3. Joy was ahead for Jesus after the Cross

         a. He would have the joy of His resurrection and ascension to the Father

         b. He would have the joy of the coming Rapture and His kingdom

         c. He would have the joy of millions saved and sharing heaven with Him

   B. We Can Look for the Potential for Good in Our Trials (v. 5)

      1. There are lessons to be learned in our trials

      2. There are changes to be made in us (Rom. 8:28–29)

      3. We need wisdom to understand what God is doing in our trials

        a.   We can ask for this wisdom and receive it

        b.   Our Lord imparts this wisdom freely to those who ask for it

    4.   God may be developing new attitudes in us through trials

    5.   God may be activating some talent in us through trials

    6.   God may impart wisdom through another person to us in our trials

C. *We Can Look to the Power of Prayer in Our Trials (vv. 6–8)*

    1.   We are invited to ask for help in trials (Heb. 4:15)

        a.   Grace to help is available in our trials

        b.   This grace is available in the time of need

    2.   God is there to hear and answer us in our trials

        a.   Consider the disciples in the storm (Mark 4:35–41)

        b.   Consider Mary and Martha at the death of Lazarus (John 11)

    3.   We can pray and ask others to pray

    4.   Faith grows through answered prayer during trials

III.   Conclusion

A. *We Can Look to the Prize That Awaits After Our Trials (v. 12)*

    1.   All our trials are temporary

    2.   Our Lord offers salvation by faith and He offers eternal rewards

B. *For Those Who Trust in Jesus, the Best Is Yet to Come*

Three Great Words for the Journey

Exodus 15

I. Introduction
A. *Moses and His People Have Miraculously Crossed the Red Sea*
   1. Israel's deliverance from slavery pictures our salvation
      a. We were slaves to sin and Satan
      b. We've been delivered by the blood of the Lamb
   2. Now the Israelites have a difficult journey ahead
      a. The Christian life is a journey
      b. There are many trials along the way
B. *We Have Great Words for the Journey: Celebrate, Innovate, Dedicate*

II. Body
A. *Celebrate (vv. 1–21)*
   1. "Then sang Moses and the children of Israel"
   2. These delivered ones had many things to celebrate
      a. They were no longer slaves; their enemies had been destroyed
      b. They were on their way to the Promised Land
   3. They chose to count their blessings and celebrate
      a. Moses led them in giving glory to God
      b. Moses reminded them the Lord was their strength
   4. What do we have to celebrate?
      a. Our sins have been forgiven; we're justified and on our way to heaven
      b. God has promised to be with us all the way
B. *Innovate (vv. 22–25)*
   1. The Israelites encountered their first serious problem on the journey
      a. The people ran out of water
      b. When they found water, it was bitter
   2. Sometimes bitter experiences make bitter people; these began to complain
   3. Moses knew where to turn in trouble; so should we

    4. God had an innovative solution to the water problem
        a. Moses was to cast a tree into the water to make it sweet
        b. This was a new approach for Moses, but it worked
    5. We ought to be innovative in evangelism and problem solving
    6. Our innovation should always be rooted in inspiration (the Bible)
    7. God's solutions to our problems will always involve the tree (the Cross)

  C. *Dedicate (vv. 26–27)*
    1. Moses called his people to new dedication (v. 26)
        a. "Diligently hearken to the voice of the LORD"
        b. "Do that which is right in his sight"
        c. "Give ear to his commandments and keep all his statutes"
    2. Healing and blessings would follow their dedication
    3. We cannot expect God's blessings apart from our full dedication

III. Conclusion
  A. *Have You Started the Journey? Have You Been Saved?*
  B. *God Wants to Meet You Where You Are and Travel with You*
  C. *God's Great Words for the Journey Will Help Along the Way*

Not Fishing? Not Following!

Mark 1:14–18

I. **Introduction**
   A. *Jesus Calls His First Disciples*
      1. Peter and Andrew were fishing
      2. "Come after me, and I will make you fishers of men"
         a. That was a clear call to faith and what it would mean to follow
         b. Following Christ would make them fishers of people
         c. Fishing for people is the most neglected of the calls of Christ
   C. *This Is a Serious Call, One That Demands Our Attention*
   D. *How Can We Become Fishers of People?*

II. **Body**
   A. *We Can Follow Christ in His Contacts with People*
      1. Jesus loved people and had time for them
         a. He loved the rich and the poor
         b. He loved the young and the old
         c. He loved the socially accepted and the outcasts
      2. He loved the woman at the well, who had a thirsty heart (John 4:5–30)
      3. He loved the ruler who was ruled by his fears (John 3:1–21)
      4. He loved the poor rich man in the sycamore tree (Luke 19:1–10)
      5. The love of Christ for people was evident in every contact
         a. If we're to become fishers of men, we must love all people
         b. Has a lack of love kept you from reaching people for Christ?
   B. *We Can Follow Christ in His Compassion on the Cross*
      1. Jesus said, "Father, forgive them," to the cursing crowd
      2. While He suffered, He won a soul
         a. The thief saw a king with a crown of thorns

47

   b. He said, "Lord, remember me" (Luke 23:42–43)

   c. The Lord said, "To day, shalt thou be with me in paradise"

  3. The pain and shame of the Cross proved His love

   a. His love reaches to every sinner

   b. His love guarantees salvation by faith alone

   c. His love is the heart of the gospel

  4. Fishing for people demands love for those we're trying to reach

  5. Without love, efforts at witnessing are worthless (1 Cor. 13)

 C. *We Can Follow Christ by Being Fully Committed to His Mission*

  1. Christ was fully committed to His Father's will (John 6:38)

   a. He came to die for sinners

   b. He came to provide eternal life

  2. Christ has commissioned His followers to carry out His mission

   a. This is clear in the Great Commission (Matt. 28:18–20)

   b. In obeying His commission, we become fishers of people

III. Conclusion

 A. *Have You Been Fishing Lately?*

 B. *If You've Not Been Fishing, You've Not Been Following*

 C. *Decide to Follow Jesus and Go Fishing Every Day*

Risking All on God

Ezra 8:21–23

I. Introduction

    A. Ezra and His People Were in Danger

        1. They experienced anxiety at the river Ahava

        2. They had reasons to fear for their lives

    B. We All Pass Through <u>Worrisome</u> Periods of Danger

        1. We experience anxiety over our adversaries: demons, disease, depression

        2. <u>Anxiety</u> robs us of joy, peace, health

    C. Where Do We Turn in Times of Danger?

II. Body

    A. Ezra Leads His People in Seeking God (v. 21)

        1. He calls for <u>fasting and prayer</u>

          a. He looks for help in this time of danger

          b. Like the psalmist, he looks up (Ps. 121)

        2. This was a time for <u>desperate praying</u>

          a. Their lives, their children, and their possessions were in danger

          b. Everything precious to them was on the line

        3. <u>Heroes of the faith</u> have sought God in desperate times

          a. David said, "Thy face, LORD, will I seek" (Ps. 27:8)

          b. Isaiah said, "With my soul will I seek Thee" (Isa. 26:9)

          c. Daniel said, "Seek by prayer . . . with fasting" (Dan. 9:3)

        4. Those who earnestly seek God find Him (Jer. 29:13)

    B. Ezra Leads His People in <u>Surrendering to God</u> (v. 22)

        1. The temptation is to <u>look to people for help</u> instead of to God

          a. The king could help them

          b. Soldiers could be their salvation

        2. But, in this case, their testimony for God was at stake

          a. They had told the king of God's power

        b.   They had testified of God's faithfulness in the past

    3.   They chose to risk all on God

    4.   Would we have dared do the same?

        a.   Do we trust God or humans when the situation is serious?

        b.   Do we expect God to come through when we need Him?

C. *God Saves Ezra and His People (v. 23)*

    1.   God meets His people where they are

        a.   He hears their prayers, as He has promised to do

        b.   He responds to their seeking hearts

    2.   This text pictures our salvation

        a.   We were in danger because of our sin

        b.   Fear gripped our hearts over the future

        c.   We sought the Lord and found Him through faith in His Son

III.   Conclusion

A. *Do You Find Yourself in a Place of Danger?*

B. *God Loves You and Will Come Through for You*

C. *Seek the Lord and His Salvation Today*

A Little Reviving

Ezra 9:8–9

I. **Introduction**
   A. *Begin With Reviewing God's Blessings*
      1. Ezra begins his prayer with thanksgiving
      2. He sets a good example for us all (Ps. 103)
   B. *Then Think About What God Has Done*
      1. Ezra chose to accentuate the positive
      2. This in spite of his many trials
   C. *Ezra Found a Little Reviving*

II. **Body**
   A. *Ezra Focused on God's Grace*
      1. "For a little space grace"
      2. Ezra and his people had been in bondage
         a. They had lived under the laws of their captors
         b. They had longed to go home and be free
         c. Ezra could have focused on their sorrows
      3. Grace allowed a remnant to return to their home, so Ezra gave thanks
      4. We also live in a space of grace
         a. We do so in spite of our sins (Rom. 3:20–23)
         b. God's grace offers us salvation (Eph. 2:8–9)
         c. The space of grace reaches from the Cross to Christ's return
      5. Have you responded in faith to God's offer of grace?
   B. *Ezra Focused on God's Faithfulness*
      1. "To give us a nail in his holy place"
         a. "Nail" refers to the remnant returning *(Scofield Reference Bible)*
         b. The number returning was small but significant
      2. God had faithfully preserved His people
      3. Ezra found reasons to rejoice in this remnant
         a. He could have grieved over those who refused to come with him
         b. He chose to rejoice in those who responded to God's call

51

        c.   We face similar choices every day. How will we respond to them?

    4.   Has God been faithful to you?

    5.   Does His faithfulness fill your heart with praise?

C. *Ezra Focused on God's Goodness*
  1. "That our God may lighten our eyes"
  2. God is the source of light and life
      a. "God is light" (1 John 1:5)
      b. Christ is the Light of the World (John 8:12)
  3. Our evil enemies are called the powers of darkness (Eph. 6:12)
  4. God is good to us and provides deliverance through His Son (Col. 1:13)

III. Conclusion

A. *Ezra Found a Little Reviving*
  1. A little reviving is worth finding
  2. Little revivals can grow into big ones

B. *Let's Follow Ezra's Focus and Expect a Revival to Begin*

Rebuilding

good
rolecut

Nehemiah 1; 2:17–20

I. Introduction

A. *Who Was Nehemiah?*
1. He was a contemporary of Ezra, another rebuilder
   a. Both lived at the end of the captivity
   b. Both were getting ready to return home
2. There were three returns: under Zerubbabel, Ezra, and Nehemiah

B. *Nehemiah Was the Rebuilder*
1. He was brokenhearted over the ruined walls of Jerusalem
2. He left an important position with the king to rebuild them
3. Churches need rebuilding after spiritual decline
4. Christians need rebuilding after backsliding and defeat

C. *How Can We Rebuild?*   *Revival*

II. Body

A. *We Can Rebuild Through Prayer (1:4–5)*
1. "Every great work of God can be traced to a kneeling figure" (Moody)
2. Nehemiah weeps, fasts, and prays
   a. He praises God for His love and power
   b. He cries out for God's help in rebuilding

Prayer
3. Plans for rebuilding may fail, but prayer prevails
4. Believing prayer places success within our reach in spite of the obstacles   *obstacles*
5. "The child of God should flee at once to Him who stills the seas" (C. H. Spurgeon)

B. *We Can Rebuild Through Confession of Sin (1:6–11)*
1. Nehemiah confessed his sins and those of his people
   a. Note how specific he was in confessing (vv. 6–7)
   b. Sins confessed are sins forgiven (1 John 1:9)
2. Confession of sin is the result of the conviction of the Holy Spirit
3. Confession of sin puts away all self-righteousness

    4. Confession of sin recognizes God's love and grace
    5. When cleansed by confession of sin, Nehemiah claimed God's promises
    6. Like Isaiah after his confession, Nehemiah was ready to serve (Isa. 6:1–8)

  C. *We Can Rebuild Through Making New Commitments (2:18–19)*
    1. "Let us rise up and build"
      a. This was a commitment linked to a challenge
      b. This was a commitment that demanded their best
      c. This was a commitment that disregarded their critics
    2. This would be a good time to make a new commitment to Christ
      a. Have you failed to carry through in the past?
      b. Confess that failure and rededicate your life to Him

III. Conclusion
  A. *When Our Hearts Are Right, We Can Rebuild with Confidence*
    1. "The God of heaven, he will prosper us" (2:20)
    2. No doubters were there; they believed God and moved ahead
  B. *God Is Always Up to the Occasion*
  C. *Are You Ready to Accept His Invitation to Rebuild?*

Celebrate Your Sources of Strength

Nehemiah 8:10; Psalm 37:39; Isaiah 30:15

I. Introduction

A. *Nehemiah Had Led His People to a Great Victory*
1. The broken wall of Jerusalem had been his burden
2. Now the wall had been repaired
   a. The people had risen above their fears
   b. They had overcome their adversaries
   c. Their labor had been rewarded

B. *Ezra Led the Dedication Service*
1. Shouts of praise were lifted to the Lord (Neh. 8:6)
2. The people were encouraged to celebrate
   a. They were told to be joyful, not solemn nor sad
   b. They were to celebrate the source of their strength

C. *We Ought to Celebrate Our Sources of Strength*

II. Body

A. *The Joy of the Lord Provides Strength (Neh. 8:10)*
1. Nehemiah and his people had faced many obstacles
   a. They could have become discouraged
   b. They could have compromised with their enemies
2. The joy of the Lord enabled them to keep building
3. We ought to be joyful for God's love, His grace, His salvation
4. The joy of the Lord will replenish our strength every day

B. *The Presence of the Lord Provides Strength (Ps. 37:39)*
1. "He is their strength in the time of trouble"
2. We all go through times of trouble
   a. "Man is born unto trouble" (Job 5:7)
   b. "Man . . . is of few days and full of trouble" (Job 14:1)
   c. "In the world ye shall have tribulation" (John 16:33)

55

    3.   Christians do not face trouble alone
        a.   "I am with you alway" (Matt. 28:20)
        b.   "I will never leave thee, nor forsake thee"
             (Heb. 13:5)
    4.   "When trouble overthrows the wicked, it only
         drives the righteous to their strong Helper, who
         rejoices to uphold them" (C. H. Spurgeon)

C. *The Promises of the Lord Provide Strength (Isa. 30:15)*
    1.   "In quietness and in confidence shall be your
         strength"
        a.   We can rest securely on the promises of God
        b.   God's promises are strong anchors in life's
             storms
    2.   Promises of salvation, fellowship, heaven, peace
         abound in the Bible
    3.   God's promises bring strength in times of waiting
         (Isa. 40:31)
    4.   Do you have a promise from God that gives you
         strength in trembling times?

III.   **Conclusion**
    A. *Let's Celebrate Our Sources of Strength*
    B. *Let's Celebrate Our Savior and His Salvation*
        1.   Discouragement drains away our strength
        2.   Faith gives the victory, enabling us to overcome
             discouragement and find peace

good

Gifts to the Church

Evangelist, Pastor, Teacher

Ephesians 4:11–12

I. Introduction
  A. *Christ Loves His Church*
  1. He is the builder of the church (Matt. 16:18)
  2. He bought the church (Eph. 5:25)
  3. He bestowed gifts on the church (Eph. 4:8)
  B. *Christ Gave Five Great Gifts to the Church*
  1. He gave apostles and prophets to establish the church (Eph. 2:20; 4:11)
  2. He gave evangelists, pastors, and teachers to develop the church (4:11–12)
  a. These are our concern today
  b. How should these three gifts affect our church?

II. Body
  A. *Evangelists Should Enlarge and Inspire the Church*
  1. Philip was the first to be called an evangelist
  a. He had been appointed a deacon (Acts 6:5)
  b. Paul called him an evangelist (Acts 21:8)
  2. Philip, the evangelist, was a soul winner (Acts 8)
  a. He had become a preacher of the gospel (8:5–7)
  b. He was directed to a seeking sinner (8:5–7)
  c. He led this seeking sinner to the Savior (8:37–39)
  3. Philip was a traveling evangelist (8:40)
  4. Evangelists win souls and motivate soul winners
  B. *Pastors Should Enrich and Exhort the Church*
  1. Pastors must lead the church as shepherds
  a. They must lead the church in Bible study (2 Tim. 2:15)
  b. They must lead the church in evangelism (2 Tim. 4:5)
  c. They must lead the church in prayer (1 Tim. 2:1–8)
  2. Pastors must love the church (1 Cor. 13)
  a. Without love, preaching is but noise
  b. Without love, leadership becomes dictatorial
  c. Without love, counseling is but futile therapy

    3. Pastors must lift the church (2 Tim. 4:2)
       a. People are often beaten down by their circumstances
       b. Pastors exhort (encourage) them, build them up

  C. *Teachers Should Instruct and Challenge the Church*
    1. The church at Antioch had many teachers (Acts 13:1)
       a. No wonder it became a great missionary church
       b. Teachers broaden the vision and understanding of believers
    2. Teachers also evangelize and bring converts to maturity
       a. Moody was led to Christ by his Sunday school teacher
       b. See how far reaching a teacher's work can become
    3. The church with effective teachers builds strong members

III. Conclusion

  A. *Churches Are Equipped by Jesus for Growth and Success*
  B. *The Gifts Given Them Enable Them to Make a Difference*

The Woman We Can't Forget

Matthew 26:6–13

I. **Introduction**
   A. *Jesus Stops at Bethany on His Way to the Cross*
      1. It is two days before Passover, the Old Testament type of His coming sacrificial death
      2. The betrayal by Judas and the Crucifixion are just ahead
   B. *Jesus Was Invited to a Meal at the House of Simon the Leper*
      1. Mary, Martha, and Lazarus were also guests (John 12:1–2)
      2. Mary's act of devotion that day has caused her to always be remembered
   C. *Mary of Bethany Gained a Place in History*

II. **Body**
   A. *She Didn't Let Others Keep Her from Coming to Christ (v. 7)*
      1. "There came unto him a woman"
      2. There were obstacles to keep Mary from coming to Jesus
         Others may hinder our app. to Jesus.
         a. She risked again leaving all the serving to Martha
         b. She did not want to intrude on Jesus and Lazarus
         c. She may have feared what others might say
      3. Many will miss heaven because of other people
         a. Are you allowing others to keep you from Christ?
         b. Are hypocrites holding you back from salvation?
         c. Have you been offended by some professing Christian?
      4. Mary overcame the obstacles and came to Jesus
      5. Follow her example and come to Jesus today
   B. *She Didn't Limit Her Consecration to Christ (v. 7)*
      1. "An alabaster box of very precious ointment"

    2. Consider what precious gifts Jesus has given to us

       a. He shed His "precious blood" (1 Peter 1:19)

       b. He has given us "precious promises" (2 Peter 1:4)

    3. Heroes of the faith held nothing back from their Lord (Heb. 11)

    4. What are you withholding from Jesus?

       a. Are you afraid to surrender all?

       b. Do you fear total devotion will cost too much?

    5. What limits are you placing on your dedication to Him?

  C. *She Didn't Listen to the Criticism of Her Care for Christ (vv. 8–9)*

    1. "This ointment might have been sold for much"

       a. A criticism was started by Judas (John 12:4–6)

       b. Others may be affected by our negative comments

    2. Critics always claim honorable reasons for their criticism

       a. Judas said his concern was for the poor

       b. In truth, he didn't care for the poor (John 12:6)

    3. Tune out the critics and serve the Lord

III. Conclusion

  A. *What Did Mary's Gift Have to Do with the Gospel (v. 12)?*

    1. This gift spoke of Christ's coming death

    2. Mary believed Christ's prophecy of His death on the Cross (v. 2)

  B. *Sharing the Gospel Is the Greatest Gift We Can Give to Our Lord*

Angels on Call

Series on the Cross and
Resurrection Begins   *Matthew 26:47–56*

I. Introduction
  A. *The Adversary and Judas Become Associated*
    1. Satan enters into Judas to betray Jesus (Luke 22:3)
    2. The betrayal and arrest of Jesus occurs in Gethsemane
    3. Jesus could have called seventy-two thousand angels to deliver Him (Matt. 26:53)
  B. *Angels and Jesus Are Associated*
    1. Angels are associated with the birth of Jesus (Luke 1:26–37; 2:1–14)
    2. Angels are present after the temptation of Jesus (Matt. 4:11)
    3. Angels are present at the resurrection of Jesus (Matt. 28:1–7)
  C. *Why Didn't Jesus Call Angels to Deliver Him?*

II. Body
  A. *The Scriptures Must Be Fulfilled*
    1. The Cross was in God's eternal plan (1 Peter 1:20)
    2. Prophecies of the Cross are found throughout the Bible
      a. Every Passover lamb pictured the slain Savior
      b. David wrote of the coming Crucifixion (Ps. 22)
      c. Isaiah described Christ's sufferings and death (Isa. 53)
      d. Zechariah wrote about Christ's wounds on the Cross (Zech. 13:6)
    3. Even the betrayal of Jesus was prophesied (Ps. 55:13)
    4. An angelic interruption of the Cross would have left us without a Savior
  B. *The Savior Must Be Forsaken*
    1. Jesus repeatedly revealed His coming betrayal
      a. "The Son of man shall be betrayed" (Matt. 17:22)

      b. "Shall deliver him to the Gentiles" (20:19)
2. Jesus told His disciples they would forsake Him (v. 1)
3. The prophets said Jesus would die alone, forsaken
      a. David said, "Despised of the people" (Ps. 22:6–8)
      b. Isaiah said, "We hid . . . our faces from him" (Isa. 53:3)
4. Jesus must even be forsaken by His Father (Ps. 22:1; Matt. 27:46)
5. Jesus was forsaken so we might never be forsaken

C. *Souls Must Be Freed from Their Sins*
1. Had angels intervened there would have been no gospel
      a. No gospel would have meant no salvation
      b. All would be lost—forever without hope
2. God's love kept Jesus on the Cross (Rom. 5:8)
      a. Angels were not summoned so we might be saved
      b. We can be clean because the angels weren't called

III. Conclusion

A. *The Call of Christ Is to Sinners Not to Angels*
B. *Have You Responded to His Call to Salvation?*
1. Has God been speaking to your heart about your sins?
2. Have others been talking to you about being right with God?
C. *Will You Respond to God's Call Today?*

The Gospel Gardens

Series on the Cross and Resurrection *Genesis 3:15;*
Matthew 26:36; John 19:41–42

I. Introduction
    A. *Gardens Reveal the Love of God*
        1. The beauty of a garden reveals a loving Designer
        2. The bounty of a garden reveals a loving Provider
    B. *Gardens Play a Role in the Gospel*
        1. The Garden of Eden was the first
        2. Jesus was betrayed in the Garden of Gethsemane
        3. Jesus was buried in the garden of the tomb
    C. *The Gospel Can Be Found in the Gardens of God*

II. Body
    A. *The Savior Was Promised in the Garden of Eden (Gen. 3:15)*
        1. After Creation, God planted a garden (2:8)
          a. It was a garden of beauty (pleasant to the eyes)
          b. It was a garden of bounty (good for food)
        2. The Garden became home for Adam and Eve
          a. All their needs were supplied from the Garden
          b. God met them in the Garden for fellowship
        3. There was but one restriction in the Garden: the forbidden tree (v. 3)
        4. Disobedience led to temptation and the Fall (vv. 4–13)
        5. God made the promise of redemption (v. 15)
        6. Christ, the promised One, would bruise the Serpent's head
    B. *The Garden of Gethsemane Sheltered the Praying Savior (Matt. 26:36)*
        1. The time to bruise the Serpent's head drew near (v. 1)
        2. Jesus entered the Garden of Gethsemane to pray
          a. Peter, James, and John accompanied Him
          b. The Savior's sorrow was poured out in the Garden
          c. Angels came to strengthen Him (Luke 22:43)

        d.   Great drops of His blood fell to the ground during His intense praying

        e.   How puny our prayers seem in comparison to His that day!

    3.   The most difficult prayer to pray is "Thy will be done"

    4.   Have we been willing to make that our prayer?

  C.   *The Garden of the Tomb Was the Place of the Powerful Savior (John 19:41–42)*

    1.   Here the Crucifixion is past

        a.   Christ has died for sinners—for you and me

        b.   Jesus is placed in Joseph's tomb in a garden

        c.   The Scriptures have been fulfilled (Isa. 53)

    2.   The garden tomb became the scene of the Resurrection

        a.   The stone closing the tomb was rolled away (20:1)

        b.   The linen clothes were there but not Jesus (20:5)

    3.   Death could not hold our powerful Savior

III.   Conclusion

  A.   *God's Gardens Reveal Our Promised, Prayerful, Powerful Savior*

  B.   *Will You Trust Him to Save You Today?*

  C.   *Will You Allow His Love to Bloom in the Garden of Your Heart?*

Resurrection Before Dawn

Series on the Cross and Resurrection   *John 20:1–2*

I. Introduction
  A. *The Crucifixion Had Brought Earth's Darkest Day*
   1. Even the light of the sun had been hidden from view
   2. Imagine the dark despair that swept in on the followers of Christ
   3. They had forgotten or doubted His promise to rise from the dead
  B. *Troubled Women Make Their Way to the Tomb*
   1. They are coming with spices to anoint the body of Jesus
   2. Mary Magdalene runs ahead of the others and arrives at the tomb before dawn
  C. *Lessons Are Drawn from Mary's Early Arrival at the Empty Tomb*

II. Body
  A. *We Ought to Come to Jesus Early (v. 1)*
   1. "The first day of the week cometh Mary Magdalene early"
   2. Why did Mary arrive early?
      a. Her broken heart required immediate attention
      b. She wanted to get to Jesus as soon as possible
   3. There are no good reasons to delay coming to Jesus for salvation
      a. "Now is the accepted time; now is the day of salvation" (2 Cor. 6:2)
      b. The longer we wait, the less likely we are to come to Him (Heb. 3:13)
      c. Every effort should be made to reach people early in life (Matt. 19:14)
   4. We should come to Jesus early to give Him our burdens (1 Peter 5:7)
   5. Rich devotional lives are developed by seeking Jesus early in the day (Ps. 63:1)
  B. *We Ought to Come to Jesus While It's Still Dark (v. 1)*
   1. "When it was yet dark"

2. Mary Magdalene knew a lot about darkness
   a. She had once been dominated by the powers of darkness
   b. She had been possessed by seven demons (Mark 16:9)
3. Jesus had introduced Mary to the light
   a. He had cast seven devils out of her, delivering her from their power
   b. Mary had learned that Jesus is the Light of the World (John 8:12)
   c. The gospel turns us from darkness to light (Acts 26:28)
   d. Those who come to Jesus no longer walk in darkness (1 Peter 2:9)
4. We cannot escape the power of darkness in our own strength
5. God will meet us in dark times and bring us light

C. *We Ought to Come to Jesus in Spite of the Obstacles (v. 1)*
   1. Mary envisioned having to overcome powerful obstacles to get to Jesus
      a. The tomb had been closed by a large stone
      b. The tomb was sealed and guarded by representatives of the Roman Empire
   2. There are always obstacles in getting to Jesus: pride, fear, selfishness, favorite sins, etc.
   3. What obstacles are keeping you from coming to Him?

III. Conclusion

A. *Those Who Come to Jesus Find the Obstacles Rolled Away (v. 1)*
   1. The stone had been rolled away from the tomb by an angel
   2. Mary found the grave empty; Christ was alive
B. *Those Who Find Christ Alive Ought to Spread the Good News (v. 2)*

From Tears to Triumph on Easter Morning

Series on the Cross and Resurrection   *John 20:11–18*

I. **Introduction**
 A. *A Woman Weeps at a Grave*
  1. Many have wept at graves throughout the centuries
  2. Jesus wept at the grave of Lazarus (John 11:25)
 B. *Mary Was Crying at an Empty Grave*
  1. The Cross and its tears were past
  2. Mary and the other women had found the grave empty
  3. Christ had risen from the dead
  4. This was a time of triumph . . . not of tears
 C. *An Angel's Question: "Why Weepest Thou?" (v. 13)*

II. **Body**
 A. *Mary Wept Because She Believed the Worst (v. 13)*
  1. She doubted the promise of the Lord
   a. Jesus had promised He would rise from the dead (John 2:19)
   b. When we doubt God's promises, we are overcome by anxiety
  2. Mary had come to the tomb to anoint the body of Jesus
   a. She had come to do the work of an undertaker
   b. Even the empty tomb hadn't convinced her Christ was alive
  3. Now Mary believed the body of Jesus had been stolen
  4. Mary believed her enemies were more powerful than her Friend   *good*
  5. We need to doubt our doubts and believe our beliefs
 B. *Mary Wept Because She Thought She Was Alone (v. 13)*
  1. Mary doubted the presence of the Lord
   a. "They have taken away my Lord"
   b. "I know not where they have laid him"
  2. Loneliness is hard to bear

          a.   No wonder Mary was weeping that first Easter morning

          b.   Jesus was there, but Mary didn't realize it

     3.   Christians are never alone (Heb. 13:5)

          a.   No one can take our Lord away (Matt. 28:18–20)

          b.   No one can take us away from our Lord (Rom. 8:38–39)

C. *Mary Wept Because She Thought Her Life Was Over (vv. 13–14)*

     1.   She now doubted the purpose of the Lord for her life

          a.   Everything had been different since she met Jesus

          b.   She had found a purpose for living at last

          c.   Now that He was gone she thought her life was over

     2.   Jesus was there all the time

          a.   He was there when Mary doubted

          b.   He was there when Mary despaired

     3.   Jesus is here today to speak to your doubts and despair

III. Conclusion

A. *Jesus Spoke to Mary and Dispelled Her Fears (vv. 15–17)*

B. *Jesus Knows About Your Tears and Fears*

C. *The Living Christ Wants to Give You Peace and a Purpose for Living*

The Risen Christ Gives Peace

Series on the Cross and Resurrection Ends   *John 20:19–26*

I. **Introduction**
   A. *Humans Search for Peace*
      1. The search has continued since Eden's fall
      2. The wicked cannot find peace (Isa. 57:21)
      3. The last days will experience false peace (1 Thess. 5:3)
   B. *Jesus Promises Peace*
      1. Isaiah made a prophecy of Christ: the Prince of Peace (9:6)
      2. Jesus promises peace: "My peace I give unto you" (John 14:27)
   C. *The Risen Christ Is the Source of Peace*

II. **Body**
   A. *We Can Have Peace When We're Afraid (v. 19)*
      1. "Where the disciples were assembled for fear of the Jews"
      2. This was a day for hallelujahs, but the disciples were in hiding
         a. Christ had risen from the grave; He was alive!
         b. The tomb was empty; the promise of resurrection fulfilled
         c. Angels had rolled the stone away, showing God's power
      3. Jesus appeared to the disciples when they were afraid
         a. The doors being shut could not keep Jesus from those He loved
         b. "No doors can shut out Christ's presence" (Matthew Henry)
      4. When Jesus comes he speaks peace to fearful hearts
      5. Faith in the crucified and risen Christ takes our fears away
   B. *We Can Have Peace When We're Apprehensive (vv. 20–21)*
      1. "He shewed unto them his hands and his side"

69

   a.   These were the hands that had been nailed to
        the cross
   b.   This was the wound in His side that confirmed
        His death to the soldiers
2.   The doubting disciples were now amazed that
     Christ was risen
   a.   What would this mean to them?
   b.   Would they be up to the responsibilities this
        would bring?
3.   Jesus speaks peace to those He is about to assign
     the task of world evangelism
   a.   "As my Father hath sent me, even so send I
        you"
   b.   They would not go in their own strength but in
        the power of the Holy Spirit
   c.   We can be at peace about the power we need
        to witness for the risen Christ
C. *We Can Have Peace When We Feel Alone (vv. 26–29)*
   1.   "And Thomas with them"
   2.   Thomas had missed the first meeting with Christ
        after His resurrection
   a.   He had doubted the word of the disciples and
        gained his name—"Doubting Thomas"
   b.   Now he meets with the believing ones, the
        only doubter among them
   c.   Thomas must have felt alone among these
        believers
   3.   Closed doors could not keep Jesus from dispelling
        the doubts of Thomas
   4.   Jesus brought proof and peace to the disciple who
        felt alone: "Be not faithless"

III. Conclusion
A. *Are You Enslaved by Fear? Trust Christ and Have
     Peace*
B. *Are You Apprehensive About Serving? Trust Christ
     and Have Peace*
C. *Do You Feel Alone? Trust Christ and Never Feel
     Alone Again*

All Things New

Revelation 21:5

I. Introduction
    A. *Everyone Likes New Things*
        1. This is what keeps the economy moving
           a. People get bored with old things and buy new ones
           b. Even antique collectors buy new old things
        2. Everything we buy finally becomes old
    B. *God Makes Things New*
        1. We discover this in the first and last books of the Bible
        2. The Bible begins and ends with a newly created paradise
    C. *What Are Some of These New Things?*

II. Body
    A. *God Makes Things New When Christ Is Received (John 1:12)*
        1. Here is the difference between receiving Christ and getting religion
           a. Religion offers a set of laws to keep
           b. Christ offers new life and the power to live it
        2. A sinner comes to faith in Christ and old things pass away (2 Cor. 5:17)
           a. That person's sins are forgiven; he or she has a new record
           b. Things that the person loved before lose their appeal
        3. Receiving Christ brings a new nature, a new hope, and a new heavenly home
        4. The new believer has a new understanding of spiritual things
        5. New things begin at the new birth (John 3:1–5)
    B. *God Will Make Things New When Christ Returns (1 Thess. 4:16–17)*
        1. Everything will become new for believers
           a. The dead in Christ will be resurrected from their graves

   b. They will have new bodies, like the resurrected
    Christ (1 John 3:2)
  2. We need new bodies
   a. These old bodies begin to deteriorate too soon
   b. We leave life much as we entered: no teeth, no
    hair, and all wrinkled
  3. Living believers will be caught up to be with
   Christ forever
   a. These fortunate Christians will never die
    (1 Cor. 15:51)
   b. They will be changed to be like Jesus in an
    instant (15:51–53)
  4. This will finally result in Christ's millennial
   reign—a reign of peace (Rev. 19–20)
 C. *God Will Make Things New When the Universe Is*
  Rebuilt (Rev. 21:1–6)
  1. "I saw a new heaven and a new earth"
  2. This last paradise will be better than the first
  3. The beauty of the earth as we know it thrills the
   soul
   a. Still there are marks of natural disasters
    through the ages
   b. The new earth will have no scars left by the
    effects of sin
  4. The new Jerusalem comes down out of heaven
   (v. 2)
  5. There's a host of wonderful "no mores" of new
   things to come (v. 4)

III. **Conclusion**
 A. *Have You Been Made New by Receiving Christ?*
 B. *Are You Ready for Christ's Return?*
 C. *Does the Anticipation of These New Things Fill You*
  with Joy?

Some Things Never Change *ideas*

Malachi 3:6

I. Introduction

A. *We Live in a Changing World*
1. Seasons change; weather patterns change
2. The boundaries and names of nations change
3. Work and ways of living change

B. *Even People Change*
1. We change physically and emotionally with the seasons of life
2. We change in our ideas, our goals, and our convictions

C. *Since God Is Unchanging, Some Things Never Change*

II. Body

A. *The Wages of Sin Will Never Change (Rom. 6:23)*
1. "The wages of sin is death"
2. "In spite of inflation, the wages of sin remain the same" (seen on a church bulletin board)
3. A warning was given in the Garden of Eden: sin will bring death
   a. Satan's lie was, "Ye shall not surely die" (Gen. 3:4)
   b. Sin brought spiritual death and, ultimately, physical death
   c. Death continues for all (Rom. 5:12–15; Heb. 9:27)
4. Every <u>funeral and cemetery</u> we pass confirms the wages of sin is death
5. Hell at the end of a sinner's life confirms the <u>wages of sin</u>
6. The death of Christ pays sin's debt and delivers believers from its wages

B. *The <u>Law of the Harvest</u> Will Never Change (Gal. 6:7–8)*
1. We reap what we sow
2. It is impossible to sow sin and reap blessings
3. Harvesttime will be both discouraging and delightful

    a. 'Those who sow to the flesh reap corruption
    b. Those who sow to the Spirit reap everlasting life
   4. Every day along life's way we're sowing
   5. What changes do you need to make in light of the coming harvest?
  C. *The Love of God Will Never Change (Rom. 5:8)*
   1. "While we were yet sinners, Christ died for us"
   2. This is the greatest love story ever told
   3. "When I have sinned, He has loved me. When I have forgotten Him, He has loved me. When in the days of my sin, I cursed Him, yet still He loved me. He loved me before I was born. Before a star began to shine He loved me. And He has never ceased to love me all these years" (C. H. Spurgeon)
   4. The Cross proves God's love
    a. God's gift of His Son guarantees eternal life for sinners
    b. There is no greater love (John 15:13)
   5. Grace delivers God's unchanging love to those who believe (Eph. 2:8–9)

III. Conclusion
  A. *These Unchanging Truths Are Life Changers*
  B. *Will You Come as a Sinner to This Unchanging Savior?*
  C. *Who Needs to Be Changed Today?*

Incapable of Loving God until
we respond to His Love for us.

Choose Life

Some good idea

Deuteronomy 30:19–20

I. Introduction

A. *Moses Gave Final Instructions to His People*
1. He is nearing the end of his life and leadership
2. He has given them many warnings and promises (Deut. 28–29)
3. Now he calls for a decision between life and death: "choose life"

B. *We Are All Faced with (This Life and Death Decision)* (v. 19)
1. "There never was, since the fall of man, more than one way to heaven. Moses meant the same way of acceptance, which Paul more plainly described" (Matthew Henry)
2. Rejecting Christ is choosing death, resulting in hopelessness and hell
3. Receiving Christ is choosing life, resulting in happiness and heaven

C. *Choosing Life Produces Three Happy Children*

must 1st Accept

II. Body

A. *Life Gives Birth to Love (v. 20)* *it's Love*
1. "That thou mayest love the LORD thy God"
2. We are incapable of loving God until we respond to His love for us
   a. We are loved in spite of our sins (1 John 4:10)
   b. Christ's death on the cross proves His love (1 John 4:10)
   c. Salvation is the result of coming in faith to our loving Lord (1 John 4:19)
3. Love for God is then the child of choosing life through the One who loves us
4. God's love enables us to love Him and others (1 John 4:11)
5. Have you been trying to love God and others without first responding to His love?

B. *Love Gives Birth to Obedience (v. 20)*
1. "That thou mayest obey his voice"

75

    2. Children who love their parents delight in obeying them

    3. We cannot obey God until we become His children
        a. We are not naturally the children of God, so we need to be born again (John 3:3)
        b. Jesus called the Pharisees children of the Devil (John 8:44)
        c. We become God's children by receiving Christ (John 1:12)

    4. Desiring to do God's will is one of the first signs of being a child of God
        a. "My sheep hear my voice and I know them and they follow me" (John 10:27)
        b. Paul's cry was, "Lord, what wilt thou have me to do?" (Acts 9:6)

    5. Do you love God and desire to do His will?

    6. Obedience should be the natural result of your salvation

  C. *Obedience Gives Birth to Opportunities*
    1. "That thou mayest cleave unto him" (v. 20)
        a. Obeying Christ enables us to walk closely with Him
        b. Obedience brings the joy of Christian service
    2. "That thou mayest dwell in the land" (v. 20)
        a. This was God's plan for Israel and His promise to Abraham
        b. God has great plans for all His children; those plans develop as we obey Him

III. Conclusion
  A. *Have You Made the Choice That Leads to Loving God?*
  B. *Has Responding to God's Love Moved You to Obey Him?*
  C. *Are You Seizing Every Opportunity to Serve Him?*

Breaking Bread

Remember this!
Communion

Acts 20:7

I. Introduction

A. *The Lord's Day Was Observed at Troas*
1. Paul shared Communion with the believers
2. It was a service of remembering and preaching
   a. Only one man was harmed by the service
   b. A man fell asleep during the sermon: be warned

B. *What Is There About Communion That Brings Us Together?*

C. *Who Is This Savior We Remember?*

II. Body

A. *We Remember Our Scriptural Savior*
1. Christ came to fulfill the Scriptures
2. The Word became flesh and dwelt among us (John 1:14)
   a. Christ fulfilled the Scriptures in His birth
   b. Christ fulfilled the Scriptures in His life
   c. Christ fulfilled the Scriptures in His death
3. This is the Christ of the gospel
   a. Christ died, was buried, and rose again according to the Scriptures (1 Cor. 15:3–4)
   b. Proclaiming this message is the reason for the existence of our church
4. The ordinances of the church present a picture of the gospel
   a. In Communion, we remember our Lord's death
   b. In baptism, we give testimony of our Lord's burial and resurrection

B. *We Remember Our Sorrowing Savior*
1. Jesus was a man of sorrows and acquainted with grief (Isa. 53:3)
2. Consider the many sorrows of Jesus
   a. He was rejected by those He came to save
   b. He was cursed and persecuted
   c. He was betrayed by Judas
3. Even today, He sorrows as He intercedes for us

        a.   He sees our sorrows and identifies with them

        b.   The compassion of Christ did not end at the Cross

C. *We Remember Our Suffering Savior*

    1.   "He was wounded for our transgressions, he was bruised for our iniquities" (Isa. 53:5)

    2.   Consider the Cross and Christ's suffering there

    3.   The Cross was no afterthought with God

        a.   Knowing the pain and suffering of the Cross, Christ came to save us

        b.   Who can understand such love?

    4.   Christ endured the suffering of the Cross that we might escape the suffering of hell

III.   Conclusion

A. *Christ Was Our Substitute*

    1.   "The LORD hath laid on him the iniquity of us all" (Isa. 53:6)

    2.   We deserved to die, but Jesus took our place

    3.   Christ became sin for us that we might be made righteous before Him (2 Cor. 5:21)

B. *Have You Made the Message of Communion Personal?*

C. *Are You Willing to Do So Today?*

Questions from the Heart of God

Malachi 1:1–8

I. **Introduction**
   A. *Who Was Malachi and What Was His Mission?*
      1. He was the last of the Old Testament prophets
      2. After Malachi there will be four hundred years of silence
   B. *Malachi's First Message Is One of God's Love (v. 1)*
      1. "I have loved you, saith the LORD"
      2. God is ever reaching out in love to lost and backslidden people
   C. *Malachi Poses Questions from God Before Prophetic Voices Cease*

II. **Body**
   A. *If I Am a Father, Where Is My Honor? (v. 6)*
      1. "Father"—what a good word!
         a. A father loves and provides
         b. A father remains faithful when others desert us
         c. Children suffer when there is no father in the home
      2. How is God our Father?
         a. On Mars Hill, Paul said we are His offspring through Creation (Acts 17:28)
         b. Not all are God's spiritual children (John 8:44)
         c. We become God's spiritual children by receiving Christ (John 1:12)
      3. We honor our heavenly Father by honoring His Son (John 5:23)
      4. We must honor our Father with our lives, not just with our lips (Mark 7:6)
      5. We can honor our Father with our substance (Prov. 3:9; Mal. 3:10)
   B. *If I Am a Master, Where Is My Fear? (v. 6)*
      1. "Master" is a word of dedication, a disciple's word
      2. "Fear" is respect, reverence, surrender
      3. The disciples followed Jesus and called Him "Master"

     a. Following Christ reveals that we regard Him as our master

     b. We follow Him because <u>we respect</u> and <u>reverence Him</u>

   4. Paul called himself a "servant of Jesus Christ" (Rom. 1:1)

   5. Who is your master? Whose servant are you?

 C. *If You Offer Sick and Blind Animals as Sacrifice, <u>Is It Not Evil?</u> (v. 8)*

   1. The priests were polluting the altar with inferior sacrifices

     a. They offered lame, sick, and blind lambs

     b. These were not really sacrifices at all

   2. Most seriously, they did not picture the coming <u>perfect Lamb of God</u>

   3. "It is evident that these understood not the meaning of the sacrifices, as shadowing forth the unblemished Lamb of God" (Matthew Henry)

   4. Christ was to be the spotless Lamb of God, shedding His precious blood (1 Peter 1:19)

   5. God has given His best for us; we ought to give our best to Him

III. Conclusion

 A. *These Three Questions Still Thunder from the Throne*

 B. *They Reveal Both the Compassion and Holiness of God*

 C. *What Is Your Answer to These Questions from the Heart of God?*

   1. Will you respond to them with a broken heart over sin?

   2. Will you present yourself as a living sacrifice to your loving Father? (Rom. 12:1–2)

A Priceless Woman

Mother's Day   *Proverbs 31:10–31*

I. **Introduction**
  A. *How Fitting It Is to Honor Mothers*
    1. Motherhood was crowned with God's approval in Eden (Gen. 1:28)
    2. Jesus chose to be born of a woman (Luke 1:30–35; Gal. 4:4–5)
  B. *Advice Is Offered for a King in Choosing a Wife*
    1. Choose a woman of virtue
    2. Choose a woman who will be a priceless wife and mother
  C. *Who Is This Priceless Woman?*

II. **Body**
  A. *She Is a Faithful Woman (vv. 11–19)*
    1. She is faithful to her husband
      a. He knows he can trust her (v. 11)
      b. Her life goal is to do him good (v. 12)
    2. She is faithful in her daily duties (vv. 13–14)
      a. She is dependable
      b. She is a hard worker
    3. She manages her time to her family's advantage (vv. 15–19)
      a. She rises early and cares for her home and family
      b. "She takes pains in her duties and takes pleasure in them" (Matthew Henry)
  B. *She Is a Caring Woman (vv. 20–25)*
    1. She cares about the needs of the poor
    2. She reaches out to the needy (serves them, helps them)
    3. She prepares for any future difficulty facing her family
      a. She makes sure her children are clothed for winter
      b. She sees that her home is an attractive place to live
    4. She cares about her husband's reputation

     a. He is respected by his peers because of her efforts

     b. He is held in high esteem because he has chosen such a good wife

  C. *She Is a Wise Woman (vv. 26–27)*

    1. "She openeth her mouth with wisdom"

     a. "The fear of the LORD is the beginning of wisdom" (Ps. 111:10)

     b. "The fear of the LORD is the instruction of wisdom" (Prov. 15:33)

    2. Here is a woman who trusts God and instructs her family to do so

    3. This wise woman has a mouth filled with praise

     a. "It will always be wise to praise our glorious Lord" (C. H. Spurgeon)

     b. She wisely finds reasons to praise while other women pout

    4. Kindness flows from the lips of this wise woman

     a. "In her tongue is the law of kindness"

     b. She speaks kindly to her husband, her children, and others

III. Conclusion

  A. *There Are Valuable Rewards for a Priceless Woman (v. 28)*

    1. Her children rise up and call her blessed

    2. Her husband praises her

  B. *Women of Faith Reap the Blessings of God (vv. 30–31)*

A Mother's Contagious Faith

Mother's Day   *2 Timothy 1:5*

I. Introduction

A. *Mothers of Faith Have Changed the Course of History*
   1. The mother of Moses spared the great deliverer's life
   2. The mother of Samuel dedicated him to the Lord before his birth
   3. The mother of John and Charles Wesley gave birth to a revival

B. *Who Was the Mother of Eunice?*
   1. Hers is not a familiar Bible name to most—Lois
   2. Lois brought faith to her daughter, Eunice
   3. Eunice brought faith to her son, Timothy, who became a blessing to Paul

C. *Faithful Mothers Start Chain Reactions of Faith*

II. Body

A. *A Mother's Faith May Spread to Her Children*
   1. We do not know when Lois came to faith in Christ
   2. We do know that at some point she trusted Him as Savior
      a. She understood she was a sinner
      b. She grasped the concept of grace
      c. She responded in faith to God's love
   3. We know her faith was genuine (unfeigned)
   4. We know she shared her faith with her daughter
   5. Eunice saw Christ in her mother and believed
   6. What are you doing to win your children to Christ?

B. *A Mother's Faith May Spread to Her Grandchildren*
   1. Eunice gave birth to Timothy
      a. Undoubtedly Lois and Eunice had high hopes for Timothy at his birth
      b. The meaning of the name that Eunice gave to her son is "honoring God"
   2. How would these two women reach young Timothy?
      a. They did so by demonstrating genuine faith in their lives

83

      b. They did so by their prayers, examples, and teaching

      c. This is still how we reach those we love for Christ

  3. Grandparents are special people to grandchildren

  4. Lois and Eunice succeeded in bringing Timothy to Christ

  5. Paul became God's answer to their prayers by leading Timothy to faith in Jesus

C. *A Mother's Faith May Spread to Future Generations*

  1. Timothy became Paul's companion in ministry

      a. Paul's letters to Timothy still spread the faith

      b. Timothy preached at Berea, spreading the faith

      c. Timothy preached at Corinth and Macedonia, spreading the faith

      d. Timothy preached at Ephesus and Rome, spreading the faith

  2. Through Timothy's life, Lois is still spreading the faith today

      a. What a thrilling thought for every mother and grandmother!

      b. A Christian mother's influence is unlimited

III. Conclusion

A. *What Part Did Your Mother Play in Your Salvation?*

B. *Are You Actively Spreading Your Mother's Faith to Others?*

What's a Missionary to Do?

Romans 10:14–15

I. Introduction

A. *This Text Explores a Great Missionary Chapter*
   1. Paul desired Israel's salvation (v. 1)
   2. Today's text is one for soul winners (vv. 9–13)

B. *These Questions Stress the Urgency of Missions*
   1. How shall they call?
   2. How shall they believe?
   3. How shall they hear?

C. *The Strategy of Missions Is <u>Sending</u> and <u>Speaking</u> (v. 15)*

D. *What Do These Sent Ones Do?*

II. Body

A. *Missionaries Travel (v. 15)*
   1. "How beautiful are the feet!"
      a. Our feet enable us to travel
      b. They take us across the street or around the world
   2. Missionary work is about going
      a. "Go ye therefore and teach all nations" (Matt. 28:18–20)
      b. "Go ye into all the world" (Mark 16:15)
      c. "Ye shall be my witnesses" (Acts 1:8)
   3. Missionary work demands a worldwide vision
   4. Missionary work calls for a concern for all lost people

B. *Missionaries Talk (v. 15)*
   1. "Of them that preach"
   2. Missionaries talk to people
      a. They talk to people in real life situations (daily contacts)
      b. They talk to people about physical and spiritual issues
   3. Missionary work is more than gathering statistics
   4. Missionary work is <u>about loving people</u>
      a. It is about meeting people where they are

   b. It is about seeing people as God sees them
  5. Missionary work is about talking to people about Christ
 C. *Missionaries Transform Lives with the Gospel (v. 15)*
  1. "Of them that preach the gospel of peace"
  2. Missionaries have a message that changes people
   a. It is a message for troubled hearts
   b. It is a message that brings peace with God
   c. It is a message that brings inner peace
  3. This message is the gospel; delivering any other message is not missionary work

III. Conclusion
 A. *What Is the Gospel? (1 Cor. 15:3–4)*
  1. Christ died for our sins according to the Scriptures
  2. Christ was buried and rose again according to the Scriptures
 B. *The Gospel Is Good News About the Gift of Eternal Life*
 C. *Have You Received This Gift? Are You Sharing This Good News?*

A Prayer for Revival

good idea

Habakkuk 3:2

I. Introduction
A. *Some Saw Habakkuk as a Prophet of Doom*
   1. He prophesied God's judgment brought by the Chaldeans (chap. 1)
   2. He prophesied God's judgment on the Chaldeans (chap. 2)

B. *Habakkuk Declared the Danger and Consequences of Sin*

C. *Habakkuk Prayed for Revival (3:2)*
   1. This prophet prayed for revival in a difficult time
   2. Let's examine his moving prayer

II. Body
A. *It Is a Prayer Rising Out of Fear*
   1. "I have heard thy speech and was afraid"
   2. Habakkuk saw judgment coming on his people
      a. Their sins were mounting and demanding judgment
      b. The Chaldeans were to be God's instruments of judgment
   3. Sin always brings severe consequences: "The wages of sin is death" (Rom. 6:23)
   4. The Cross declares the seriousness of sin
   5. Are there sins in our lives that may bring judgment?
      a. Consider the violence and immorality on every side
      b. Think of how the abortion tragedy appears to God
   6. Are we concerned enough about our sins to pray for revival?
   7. Revival or retribution—which will it be?

B. *It Is a Prayer Requesting Revival*
   1. "Oh LORD, revive thy work"
   2. Habakkuk sees revival as their only hope
      a. He believes revival must come from God
      b. He is pleading for Holy Spirit conviction of sin

87

        c.   He is praying for people to repent . . . to turn to God

    3.   Habakkuk cries out for revival to arrive on time
        a.   "In the midst of the years"
        b.   He sees the countdown to judgment proceeding

    4.   Let's add urgency to our prayers for revival
    5.   May God awaken us to the importance of revival in our time

C.   *It Is a Prayer Respecting the Wrath of God*
    1.   Note Habakkuk's concern: "in wrath remember mercy"
        a.   He sees God's wrath is on its way
        b.   He hears the march of Chaldean warriors
        c.   He fears the devastation of divine judgment
    2.   The wrath of God is as real today as in Habakkuk's time (Rom. 1:18)
    3.   This should be a wake-up call to us all

III.   Conclusion
    A.   *Habakkuk Regarded Mercy as Their Only Hope*
        1.   The mercy of God is our only hope . . . and God is merciful
        2.   The gospel announces God's mercy to us all
    B.   *Will We Respond to God's Mercy in Time?*

God Wants Your Body

Memorial Day   *Romans 12:1*

I. Introduction

A. *This Text Is a Passionate Plea from Paul*
1. "I beseech you therefore, brethren"
    a. "I beg of you, please" (Wuest)
    b. Paul begs his readers to present their bodies to God
2. "By the mercies of God"
    a. Paul's bold call was based on all that precedes it
    b. God's mercies should move us to respond to this call

B. *How Do We Know God Is Interested in Our Bodies?*

II. Body

A. *Note the Creation of the Body (Gen. 2:7, 21–22)*
1. It is the great work of Creation
    a. God speaks and light appears
    b. God speaks and the earth and seas are formed
    c. God speaks and the earth becomes fruitful and populated by animals
2. The creation of man was different
    a. Man was created from the dust of the ground
    b. Humans called for special care by the Creator—His masterpiece
3. The creation of woman occurred from the rib of Adam
4. The characteristics of our bodies were given to fulfill God's plan
5. Christ chose a body as His vehicle of redemption
B. *Attention Should Be Given to the Care of Our Bodies (1 Cor. 6:19–20)*
1. The Christian's body is the temple of God
    a. This demands respect and care of our bodies
    b. The believer's body belongs to the Lord
2. Some are more concerned about care for the church building than for the care of their bodies

       a. Church buildings are but meeting places

       b. "Our bodies are the dwelling places of God" (A. W. Tozer)

  3. This ought to determine what we take into our bodies and how we care for them

  4. We are saved by grace but can shorten our lives by mistreating our bodies

       a. Tobacco won't send us to hell but may harm our bodies

       b. Alcohol won't send us to hell but can ruin our health

       c. Gluttony won't send us to hell but is a major killer

C. *There Is a Coming Resurrection of Our Bodies (1 Cor. 15:51–52)*

  1. God is going to bring our bodies out of their graves

  2. Christ came out of the grave bodily to guarantee our resurrection

  3. The grave of a Christian is a place of anticipation

  4. At the Resurrection, we will be like Jesus (1 John 3)

III. Conclusion

A. *We Are to Present Our Bodies to Christ as Living Sacrifices*

  1. This calls for complete surrender

  2. We are to keep our bodies morally clean

B. *We Are to Regard Our Bodies as Holy and Acceptable to God*

C. *Presenting Our Bodies to God Is the Intelligent Thing to Do*

Remembering Sacrifices of Love

1 Chronicles 11:15–19

I. Introduction

    A. *Memorial Day Is a Time to Remember*

        1. Let us remember those who sacrificed to keep us free

        2. Let us remember those who sacrificed to raise us

            a. Remember the sacrifices to feed and clothe us

            b. Remember the sacrifices to protect and educate us

        3. These are all sacrifices of love

    B. *Remember David and His Mighty Men*

        1. These men were loyal in protecting him from Saul

        2. These men were willing to give their lives for him

        3. Three captains visit David while he was in hiding from Saul's soldiers

II. Body

    A. *David Desired Water from the Well in Bethlehem (v. 17)*

        1. Bethlehem had been David's hometown

            a. He had tended sheep on the hillsides there

            b. He had been anointed king there by Samuel

        2. Memories are powerful motivators

            a. David remembered the water from Bethlehem's well

            b. He longed for a taste of home

            c. "Oh that one would give me drink"

        3. Do you long for a taste from a better time?

        4. Do you thirst for a return of better days?

    B. *David's Men Dared to Risk Everything to Get Him a Drink (v. 18)*

        1. Bethlehem was occupied by David's enemies

        2. Three of David's captains set out to get him a drink

            a. They placed their lives in jeopardy

            b. They broke through the lines of the enemy

            c. They brought water to David from Bethlehem's well

      3.   Jesus broke through enemy lines to bring us living water
          a.   His death and resurrection provide the water of life
          b.   We're offered refreshing water from Bethlehem's well
      4.   We should remember those who sacrificed so we might live and be free
      5.   We're in debt to those who've made sacrifices of love

  C. *David's Devotion Moved Him to Make a Sacrifice of Love (vv. 18–19)*
      1.   David couldn't drink the water brought to him
          a.   He remembered the cost and poured out the water
          b.   This water seemed to him to be the price of blood
          c.   The sacrifice of his captains moved him to sacrifice
      2.   Does the memory of sacrifices of love move you?
      3.   How does the memory of the sacrifice of Christ affect you?

III. Conclusion
  A. *Remembering Sacrifices of Love Ought to Change Us*
      1.   Will we be different because we've stopped to remember?
      2.   Will we value freedom and salvation more highly?
  B. *What Sacrifices of Love Will Now Appear in Our Lives?*

The Night of Terror

Daniel 5

I. **Introduction**
  A. *It Was Party Time in Babylon*
   1. King Belshazzar planned a party to remember
   2. The great banquet hall was filled with the who's who in Babylon
     a. The king's princes, his lords, his wives, and his concubines all came
     b. Wine flowed freely, leading to irreverence and shame
  B. *Belshazzar's Party Turned from Revelry to Regret*
   1. The hand that wrote the Ten Commandments wrote on the king's wall
   2. Daniel was called to interpret the message; he knew his Father's handwriting
   3. The mood was changed from feasting and fun to fear, from revelry to remorse
   4. This would be Belshazzar's last night on earth
  C. *It Turned from a Night of Triumph to a Night of Terror*

II. **Body** *Here is a way that seems right unto—*
  A. *It Was the Terror of a Wasted Life (vv. 17–24)*
   1. Belshazzar had lived his entire life without getting right with God
   2. He had seen Nebuchadnezzar's example and heard his warning (Dan. 4)
     a. Nebuchadnezzar had been humbled by God until he turned to Him
     b. The warning was "Those that walk in pride he is able to abase" (4:37)
   3. Belshazzar had invested his life in things that pass away and now faced eternity empty-handed
   4. He had time for pleasure, time for business, but no time for God; how sad!
   5. "What shall it profit a man, if he shall gain the whole world?" (Mark 8:36)
  B. *It Was the Terror of the Wrath of God (vv. 25–28)*

93

    1.   "Thou art weighed in the balances, and art found wanting"

    2.   The patience of God had been exhausted

        a.   Belshazzar's kingdom was finished; it would end that night

        b.   Sin finally catches up to us, as it did with Belshazzar

    3.   Moses wrote about the wrath of God (Deut. 9:19–20)

    4.   Paul wrote about the wrath of God (Rom. 1:18)

    5.   John wrote about the wrath of God (John 3:36; Rev. 14:19–20)

    6.   How does one escape the wrath of God?

        a.   Come to Jesus who endured the penalty of our sins on the Cross

        b.   Those who place faith in God's Son are delivered from God's wrath

  C. *It Was the Terror of a Sinner's Death (v. 30)*

    1.   Death had been the farthest thing from Belshazzar's mind when the party started

        a.   This had been a night for dancing and drinking, not for death

        b.   But death was on its way to Belshazzar's party and arrived that night

    2.   "In that night was Belshazzar . . . slain"

    3.   Death is on its way to your house and mine (Heb. 9:27)

        a.   Even kings and earth's most successful face death and leave all behind

        b.   There is terror in facing death unprepared for heaven and bound for hell

III. Conclusion

  A. *Jesus Died and Rose Again to Bring Salvation to All*

  B. *Trusting Christ Brings Purpose to Life and Assurance of Heaven*

  C. *Haven't You Been on the Road to Hell Long Enough?*

Enoch: The Preacher with One Message

Jude 14–15

I. **Introduction**
   A. *Here Are Some Interesting Facts About Enoch*
      1. He walked with God (Gen. 5:24)
      2. He didn't die (Gen. 5:24; Heb. 11:5)
      3. He was a prophet and preacher (Jude 14–15)
      4. He will be martyred during the Tribulation (Rev. 11)
   B. *What Was Enoch's Message?*
      1. It was a message about the Second Coming of Christ
      2. It was a message about the seriousness of sin
      3. It was a message about God judging sinful speech
      4. It was a message by a man who practiced what he preached
   C. *Enoch Preached a Timely Message*

II. **Body**
   A. *It Was a Good Message for Enoch's Time*
      1. Enoch lived during the ungodly time before the Flood
         a. Violence was increasing; storm clouds of judgment were gathering
         b. Ungodliness was common, and his message addressed the problem
      2. Enoch kept walking with God and was blessed
         a. His son Methuselah lived 969 years
         b. His great-grandson Noah found grace and saved the race
      3. Enoch's message was not popular among his contemporaries
   B. *It Will Be a Good Message for the Tribulation Time (Rev. 11)*
      1. After the Rapture of the church, the Tribulation begins
         a. This will be earth's most terrible time (Matt. 24:21)

        b.   It will be a time of wickedness, violence, and sacrilege

   2.   Two prophets arrive on the scene, preaching and pronouncing judgment

        a.   Elijah and Enoch will come back to preach and die

        b.   The two who escaped death will then experience it (Heb. 9:27)

        c.   Only the raptured church truly escapes death (1 Cor. 15:51–52)

   3.   See how fitting Enoch's message will be for the Tribulation (Jude 14–15)

        a.   It announces the second coming of Christ with His church

        b.   It warns that Christ's coming will bring judgment on sinners

        c.   It carries a theme of the ruling Christ as He establishes His kingdom

  C. *It Is a Good Message for Our Time*

   1.   We need to stress the neglected message of Christ's return

        a.   This message adds urgency to the preaching of the gospel

        b.   This message purifies the lives of believers (1 John 3:2)

   2.   Like Enoch, we need to stress the seriousness of sin

   3.   In an age of compromise, we need to awaken people to God's holiness

III. Conclusion

  A. *Enoch's Powerful Message Grew Out of Walking with God*

   1.   What secrets Enoch learned during his walk with God!

   2.   His communion with his Lord made him a man ahead of his time

  B. *We Must Walk with God in Order to Reach the People of Our Time*

Five Life-Changing Words

Isaiah 6:1–8

I. Introduction

A. *Millions of Christians Live Below Their Potential*
1. They are caught in ruts of unchanging routines
2. They are busy but feel their lives are barren
3. They are active but feel they accomplish little

B. *What Is Missing from the Lives of These Discontents?*
1. They have never experienced the adventure of full surrender
2. They are missing the joy of involvement in the greatest work on earth
3. They need to say with Isaiah, "Here am I; send me"

C. *How Can We Make These Five Words Life Changers for Us All?*

II. Body

A. *We Must See God as He Is (vv. 1–4)*
1. Isaiah lived in a wicked period in his nation's history
   a. His people had forsaken the Lord; violence filled the land
   b. Immorality was rampant; alcohol flowed freely
2. King Uzziah had been Isaiah's hope for the nation; then he died
   a. Now Isaiah realized his only hope must be in the Lord
   b. Politicians are unable to solve root problems; only God can do this
3. At this panic point, Isaiah was given a vision of God in all His holiness
4. The holiness of God is revealed throughout the Bible, especially at the Cross
5. Changing views of sin do not change God's holiness

B. *We Must See Ourselves as We Are (vv. 5–7)*
1. Isaiah experienced old-fashioned conviction of sin

         a. He had been made aware of the holiness of God

         b. This made him aware of his own sinfulness

    2. "Woe is me!"

         a. "I am undone"

         b. "I am a man of unclean lips"

         c. "I dwell in the midst of a people of unclean lips"

    3. How long has it been since you measured yourself by God's perfect standard?

         a. Have you been excusing your sins?

         b. Have you been comparing yourself to others and looking good?

    4. We need to confess our sins and be made clean (1 John 1:9)

C. *We Must See the World as God Sees It (v. 8)*

    1. "Whom shall I send, and who will go for us?"

    2. A lost and dying world was the reason for God's call

    3. Five words that changed Isaiah's life: "Here am I; send me"

         a. Isaiah's response launched him on a great adventure

         b. He would spend the rest of his life telling people about God

    4. Ask God to enable you to see lost people as He sees them

III. Conclusion

A. *What Is Your Answer to God's Challenging Call?*

B. *Isaiah's Five-Word Answer Gave Him a Purpose for Living*

C. *Make Isaiah's Commitment and Life Will Never Be Boring Again*

Standing Before the King

I. Introduction
   A. *The Gospel Is for Everyone*
   1. It is needed equally by the rich and the poor, the exalted and the outcasts
   2. We are all sinners, so we all will perish without the Savior (Rom. 3:23; 6:23)
   B. *Paul, the Prisoner, Stands Before Agrippa, the King*
   1. Felix had left Paul in prison to please his accusers
   2. Festus couldn't find a charge to place against Paul
   3. Now Agrippa, his wife, Bernice, and Festus listen as Paul tells his story to them
   C. *Hear What Paul Said While Standing Before the King*

II. Body
   A. *Jesus Changed the Destination of My Soul (vv. 3–15)*
   1. Paul early on had concern about his soul
      a. He was strict in the religion of his youth
      b. He lived as a Pharisee, trying to keep the law
   2. Paul persecuted Christians to gain favor with God
      a. He thought God would be pleased with his opposition to Jesus
      b. He had believers thrown into prison and was glad when they were executed
   3. Then came that decision day on the road to Damascus
      a. At noon a light brighter than the sun illuminated the road
      b. Paul heard a voice and knew it was the voice of God
      c. He learned the voice was that of Jesus and received Him as his Lord
   B. *Jesus Changed the Direction of My Life (vv. 16–25)*
   1. Paul was commissioned for a life of service to Christ
      a. "To make thee a minister and a witness"
      b. Paul ministered to open the eyes of those in spiritual darkness

       c. Paul ministered to turn people from the power of Satan to the power of God

       d. Paul ministered to bring people forgiveness of sins and an inheritance with the saved

   2. Paul was not disobedient to this heavenly call

   3. His obedience had brought him to this place and to the hands of his accusers

   4. When Paul began to fulfill his call, trouble came

       a. Enemies of the gospel tried to kill him

       b. Still, Paul kept preaching about the death and resurrection of Christ

   5. Paul seized this opportunity to explain the gospel to the king

C. *Jesus Changed the Desires of My Heart (vv. 26–29)*

   1. Paul's former desire had been to do away with Christians and their message

   2. Now preaching the gospel of Christ had become his passion

       a. Place Paul anywhere and he will tell others of God's love

       b. He will explain what happened at his conversion

   3. Paul longed for King Agrippa, his wife, Bernice, and Festus to know Jesus

   4. What is the driving desire of your heart? Is it to lead others to Christ?

III. Conclusion

A. *What About the Destination of Your Soul?*

B. *King Agrippa Was Almost Persuaded to Become a Christian*

C. *Those Who "Almost Believe" Are Lost*

The Father Who Felt Everything Was Against Him

Father's Day   *Genesis 42:36–38*

I. Introduction
   A. *Remember the Sad Story of Jacob and Joseph*
      1. Jacob had twelve sons and especially loved Joseph
      2. Joseph had been sold into slavery by his jealous brothers
      3. Jacob thought Joseph was dead
   B. *Joseph Had Become Second in Command in Egypt*
      1. A famine sent Jacob's sons (except Benjamin) to Egypt to get food
      2. Joseph, who was in charge of distributing food, had a plan to bring his family to him
         a. Simeon was held hostage in Egypt
         b. Benjamin must be brought to Egypt in order for Simeon to be set free
      3. Jacob lamented, "All these things are against me"
   C. *Why Did Jacob Utter This Faithless Cry?*

II. Body
   A. *Jacob Was Weary*
      1. The years had taken their toll on this tired father
      2. The supposed death of Joseph caused him great grief
      3. Jacob had experienced God's love and faithfulness in years past
         a. He dreamed of a ladder to heaven (Gen. 28:11–12)
         b. God promised Jacob blessings to come (Gen. 28:13–15)
         c. Jacob met with angels; he received his new name (Gen. 32)
      4. Fatigue from grief and problems can cause our faith to falter, but God is faithful
   B. *Jacob Was Worried*
      1. Losing Joseph and Simeon troubled Jacob
         a. He envisioned Benjamin being lost like his brothers

           b.   Anxiety gripped his heart and weakened his faith

      2.   Fear and faith are opposites

           a.   Jacob felt God was against him and acted accordingly

           b.   "My son shall not go down with you" (v. 38)

      3.   Fear keeps us from receiving God's best

      4.   Faith enables us to give our worries to Jesus (1 Peter 5:7)

      5.   When we feed our faith on God's Word, our fears starve to death (Rom. 10:17)

  C. *Jacob Was Wrong*

      1.   Things would turn out much better than he expected

      2.   God had been at work on Jacob's behalf

           a.   Joseph was alive and thriving

           b.   By sending Benjamin, Jacob would see Joseph again

      3.   Joseph would provide food and a home for Jacob's family

      4.   Joseph would care for Jacob in his old age

      5.   All things weren't against Jacob after all

III.   **Conclusion**

  A. *Joseph Pictures Jesus, Our Savior and Provider*

  B. *We Should Flee to Jesus When Weary and Worried*

      1.   Jesus meets us in all our difficulties

      2.   He makes everything work together for our good (Rom. 8:28)

The Man Who Couldn't Be Stopped

I. Introduction

A. *Paul's Destination Was Jerusalem*
   1. He longed to minister in that historic city
   2. He hoped to arrive by Pentecost (v. 16)
B. *Paul Received Many Warnings of Trouble Along the Way*
   1. Bonds and afflictions awaited him in Jerusalem
   2. These warnings couldn't stop him from reaching his destination
   3. "None of these things move me"
C. *What Motivated Paul to Head into Danger?*

II. Body

A. *He Was Determined to Complete His Ministry*
   1. At conversion, Paul was called to the ministry (Acts 9)
      a. Meeting Christ on the Damascus road changed him
      b. "What wilt thou have me to do?" meant full surrender
   2. Paul's ministry meant more to him than life
      a. "Neither count I my life dear"
      b. His life had been in jeopardy many times
   3. Reaching souls had become Paul's passion
      a. He used every means possible (1 Cor. 9:22)
      b. He ministered publicly and in homes (Acts 20:20)
   4. Paul preached to both Jews and Gentiles (Acts 20:21)
B. *He Was Committed to Fulfilling His Mission*
   1. Paul's goal was to finish well (v. 24)
      a. He wasn't satisfied with only past accomplishments
      b. There was no resting on his laurels
      c. He seized each day for ministry
   2. Paul believed God's plan reached to the end of his life

      a. He wanted to finish his course with joy

      b. He guarded against final failure (1 Cor. 9:27)

    3. Paul longed to complete his divine calling in delight

    4. What are you doing about finishing your course with joy?

C. *Paul Was Eager to Deliver His Message*

    1. Paul's purpose was "to testify the gospel of the grace of God"

    2. Paul never got over glorying in the miracle of grace

    3. The persecutor of Christians had been saved by grace

    4. Paul wanted to go to Jerusalem to explain grace

      a. Grace made salvation a gift

      b. Grace made legalism obsolete

      c. Grace was made possible by Christ's sacrifice for us

III. Conclusion

    A. *No Wonder Paul Couldn't Be Stopped*

    B. *We Have the Same Message to Deliver*

    C. *What's Stopping Us from Carrying Out Our Call?*

John's Great Goal

John 3:30

I. Introduction
A. *Meet John the Baptist: The Man Sent from God*
   1. Isaiah prophesied concerning John (Isa. 40:35)
   2. John's birth was a miracle
      a. The angel announced John's birth to Zacharias (Luke 1:5–25)
      b. John was born and named (Luke 1:57–64)
B. *Zacharias Had a Vision Concerning John (Luke 1:67–80)*
   1. John was to be the prophet of the Highest (v. 76)
   2. He was to prepare the way of the Lord (v. 76)
   2. He was to bring the message of salvation (v. 77)
C. *John's Goal Was That Christ Must Increase; He Must Decrease*

II. Body
A. *John's Goal Was Biblical*
   1. John was to be a voice (Isa. 40:3–5)
      a. His voice was to announce the coming Savior
      b. His voice was to announce the seriousness of sin
      c. His voice was to announce the glory of God
   2. Christ was coming as the Word
      a. A voice is heard and gone
      b. A word remains after the voice is silent
   3. John came to bear witness of the Light of the World (John 8:12)
B. *John's Goal Was Based on the Deity of Christ*
   1. John said Jesus existed before him (John 1:15)
   2. John said Jesus was superior to Moses (John 1:17)
   3. John said Jesus would show them the Father (John 1:18)
   4. John said Jesus held a higher position
      a. He saw Jesus fulfilling all Old Testament sacrifices
      b. He called Jesus the "Lamb of God" (John 1:29)

         c.   He identified Jesus as the one to take away our sins

   C.   *John's Goal Was Best for His Followers*

      1.   John's disciples had concerns about Jesus (John 3:26)

         a.   Jesus was baptizing more people than John

         b.   The crowds of Christ were increasing

      2.   John seized a teaching moment

         a.   God is in charge of everything (John 3:27)

         b.   "I am not the Christ" (John 3:28)

         c.   "I am sent before him" (John 3:28)

      3.   John spoke of the Bridegroom, His bride, and His friends (John 3:29)

      4.   Others are helped when we give Christ first place

      5.   Is your pride keeping someone from coming to Jesus?

III.   Conclusion

   A.   *Does Christ Have First Place in Your Life?*

   B.   *Do You Long to Have the Place of Honor and Praise?*

   C.   *Are You Willing to Decrease That Christ May Increase?*

John the Baptist's Down Day

Matthew 11:1–11

I. Introduction

A. *John the Baptist Was the Bold Preacher of Repentance*
   1. Crowds gathered to hear him call for repentance
   2. Even Herod came to hear John denounce sin
      a. John was fearless, sparing no favorites in his audience
      b. He rebuked the king and landed in jail
B. *In Prison, John's Faith Faltered*
   1. He began to wonder if Jesus was really the Savior
   2. He sent two of his disciples to Jesus to find out for sure
C. *Why Did John Doubt and How Did Jesus Drive Away His Doubts?*

II. Body

A. *John's Doubts Are a Warning to Us All*
   1. John's birth and life had been miraculous
      a. His birth was foretold by an angel (Luke 1:13)
      b. His ministry had been prophesied by Isaiah (Isa. 40:3–5)
   2. John's ministry demonstrated God's power and approval
      a. Many repented and were baptized
      b. John baptized Jesus (Matt. 3:13)
         (1) He saw the Spirit of God descend like a dove
         (2) He heard God's voice from heaven approving His Son
   3. John's doubts prove we must all guard against unbelief
B. *John's Doubts Warn Us of the Power of Depression*
   1. Consider John's amazing two-part question (Matt. 11:3)
      a. "Art thou he that should come?"
      b. "Do we look for another?"
   2. These questions are incredible after all John had seen and experienced

107

      3. Depression can make the strongest weak
         a. John was depressed about what had happened to him
         b. He was depressed about what might happen to him
         c. Regrets and fears are among depression's most common causes
      4. Are you bothered by these troublesome twins?

C. *John's Doubts Were to Be Overcome by Looking to Jesus*
      1. Jesus sent John an answer to build his faith
         a. The blind were given sight; the lame could walk; the deaf could hear
         b. The dead were being raised; the poor were hearing the gospel
      2. These demonstrations of the power of Christ were to banish John's depression
         a. No regrets, John, everything you said about Jesus was true (John 10:41)
         b. No fears, John, your future is in His loving hands; the best is yet to come
      3. Three words dissolve our doubts: "Looking unto Jesus" (Heb. 12:2)

III. Conclusion

A. *Jesus Didn't Condemn John for His Doubts*
B. *Jesus Understood and Demonstrated His Love to John (Matt. 11:11)*
      1. "When John the Baptist said his worst about Jesus, Jesus said His best about John" (Vance Havner)
      2. We ought to look for the best in others

National Blessings

Independence Day   *Psalm 33:12*
Series in Psalms Begins

I. Introduction

    A. *These National Hymns Plead for Blessings*
        1. "God Bless America"
        2. "America the Beautiful" (God shed His grace on thee)
        3. "America" (Protect us by Thy might, great God our king)

    B. *Will God Answer the Prayers of These Patriotic Hymns?*
        1. It depends upon the conscience and conduct of the nation (Prov. 24:34)
            a. Righteousness exalts a nation
            b. Sin is a reproach to any people
        2. It depends upon the nation's response to Christ and His Word

    C. *Let Us Issue a Call to National Revival*

II. Body

    A. *We Need a Revival Born in Prayer*
        1. "If my people . . . will humble themselves and pray" (2 Chron. 7:14)
        2. We have enough programs
            a. Strategies for church growth abound . . . and sell
            b. Programs prove what planning can do; prayer proves what God can do
        3. Consider the praying of the early church
            a. They prayed before Pentecost (Acts 1:14)
            b. There was mighty power in the church through prayer (Acts 4:31–33)
        4. Every great revival has begun in prayer

    B. *We Need a Revival That Brings Holy Living*
        1. Revival comes when people see sin as serious
        2. We've wandered far from God and His holy standards
            a. What's in your life that you once considered sinful?

       b.   We've become so tolerant of sin, we've nearly toppled

       c.   It's time for a return to biblical convictions

   3.   How can God bless America?

       a.   It is a land of immorality and broken homes

       b.   It is a land of violence and lack of respect for life (abortion, euthanasia, murder)

   4.   This return to righteousness must begin in the church

   5.   Let the line between the church and the world be clear again

C.   *We Need a Revival That Bursts Forth in Evangelism*

   1.   All true revivals have brought sinners to Christ

       a.   Evangelism is the missing word in the church today

       b.   Where have all the evangelists gone?

   2.   Let preaching on the Cross produce a passion for souls

   3.   Let sermons on hell show the cost of being lost

   4.   Let altars be filled with seeking sinners

III.   Conclusion

A.   *Can This Kind of Awakening Come to Our Land Today?*

   1.   Why not? Our Lord is unchanged

   2.   God still answers prayer

B.   *God's Blessings Flow When We Are Ready to Receive Them*

Prayer and Protection

I. Introduction
- A. *David Lived a Dangerous Life*
  1. He faced the giant Goliath, and he fled from Saul, who tried to kill him
  2. Here his son Absalom had rebelled against him
- B. *We All Face Many Dangers*
  1. Diseases that threaten our lives
  2. We face enemies, criminals, drunk drivers, angry people
- C. *Where Can We Turn for Protection?*

II. Body
- A. *David Turned to His Lord in Prayer (vv. 1–3)*
  1. This troubled father turned to his heavenly Father
     - a. "LORD, how are they increased that trouble me"
     - b. David's prayer is a good example for desperate parents
  2. Public opinion discounted prayer as being helpful
     - a. "There is no help for him in God"
     - b. Does this sound like the reaction of your friends?
  3. David saw the Lord as his shield, his protector
     - a. "But thou, O LORD, art a shield for me"
     - b. He tuned out the doubters and believed God
  4. Some pray and believe and receive
  5. Some pray and doubt and go without
- B. *David Found That God Answers Prayer*
  1. "I cried unto the LORD . . . and he heard me"
  2. "We need not fear a frowning world while we rejoice in a prayer-hearing God" (Spurgeon)
  3. Praying people are in good company
     - a. Moses prayed and the Red Sea opened
     - b. Joshua prayed and the walls of Jericho fell down
     - c. Daniel prayed and the lions couldn't harm him
     - d. Paul and Silas prayed and were freed from prison

       4.   Keep on praying; God hears and will answer in His time

  C. *David's Prayer Brought Protection and Peace (vv. 5–8)*
   1. "I laid me down and slept"
   2. "David reclined his head on the bosom of his God, slept happily beneath the wing of Providence in sweet security, and then awoke in safety" (Spurgeon)
   3. "I will not be afraid" (v. 6)
      a. The size of his problems meant nothing now
      b. He knew God was bigger than them all

III.   Conclusion

  A. *God Is Able to Protect Us*
   1. He possesses all power in heaven and on earth (Matt. 28:18–20)
   2. In Christ's death and resurrection, He overcame all His foes

  B. *Surrender All to Our Victorious Lord and Have Peace*

Priorities in Prayer

Series in Psalms   *Psalm 5:1–3*

I. Introduction
   A. *The Psalmist Sorts Out His Priorities*
      1. He decides God will have the best hours of the day
      2. He offers God the mornings of his life
   B. *Spurgeon Spoke on the Importance of Starting the Day with God*
      1. "An hour in the morning is worth two in the evening"
      2. "While the dew is on the grass let grace drop on the soul"
   C. *Morning Prayer Brightens the Whole Day*

II. Body
   A. *Prayer Takes Preparation (v. 1)*
      1. "Give ear to my words, O LORD"
         a. Prayer is more than a recitation
         b. Prayer cries out to God, expecting Him to hear
      2. "Consider my meditation"
         a. True prayer is deeper than our words
         b. Prayer is thoughtful, flowing from the heart
      3. The psalmist didn't want to waste his words
         a. He was determined to have his prayer reach God
         b. "Do we not miss much of the sweetness and power of prayer because we do not prepare our hearts to pray? We should begin to pray before we kneel down" (Spurgeon)
   B. *Prayer Is a Personal Relationship (v. 2)*
      1. "My King, and my God"
      2. Prayer is not unheard conversation with an unknown God
         a. It is a personal conversation with our living Lord
         b. Consider the Twenty-third Psalm: "The LORD is *my* shepherd"
      3. Think of Jesus praying in Gethsemane (Matt. 26:36–39)
      4. Prayer is a child talking to his or her Father

113

          a. We become the children of God by faith (John 1:12)

          b. Are you a member of the family of God?

  C. *Pray with a Positive Outlook (v. 3)*

     1. "I will direct my prayer unto thee, and will look up"

     2. This kind of praying reaches the throne of God

          a. All limits of expectation are removed

          b. Prayer is a petition to our omnipotent God

          c. No wonder prayer makes all things possible

     3. Seeking God early starts the day in faith instead of fear

     4. Morning prayers lift the clouds and let the sunshine in

III. Conclusion

  A. *What Are Your Priorities?*

  B. *Who Has First Place in Your Life?*

  C. *What Are Your Expectations When You Pray?*

     1. "Let holy preparation link hands with patient expectation, and we shall have far greater answers to our prayers" (Spurgeon)

Lord, Have Mercy!

Series in Psalms   *Psalm 6*

I. Introduction
    A. The First of the Penitential Psalms
        1. David has now tasted the bitterness of sin
        2. He expresses sorrow, humiliation, and the fear of God's wrath
        3. We can all identify with him
    B. David Cries for Mercy and Receives It
        1. "Have mercy upon me, O LORD" (v. 2)
        2. "The LORD hath heard my supplication" (v. 9)
    C. Who Obtains Mercy from the Lord?

II. Body
    A. Those Who Realize They Need Mercy Receive It (vv. 1, 3, 6)
        1. "O LORD, rebuke me not in thine anger"
        2. David doesn't deny his sinfulness
            a. He confesses his sins
            b. He admits he is worthy of rebuke and chastening
        3. Conviction of sin is the first evidence of need
            a. David's soul was so troubled he wept all night over his sins
            b. "When the soul is troubled, this is agony" (Spurgeon)
        4. We are all guilty before God (Rom. 3:10–23)
            a. Have you faced your guilt?
            b. Do you realize you need God's mercy?
    B. Those Who Remember That Mercy Is Available Receive It (vv. 2, 4)
        1. "Save me for thy mercies' sake"
        2. How do we know God's mercy is available?
            a. "The LORD is . . . of great mercy" (Num. 14:18)
            b. "His mercy endureth forever" (1 Chron. 16:34)
            c. "He delighteth in mercy" (Micah 7:18)
            d. "God, who is rich in mercy" (Eph. 2:4)

    3. The mercy seat in the tabernacle revealed God's mercy (Exod. 25:17)

       a. The mercy seat was sprinkled with blood (Lev. 16:15)

       b. Mercy flows from the Cross where Jesus died

    4. The gospel declares God's mercy is available to all

  C. *Those Who Request Mercy Receive It (vv. 2, 9)*

    1. "Have mercy upon me, O LORD"

    2. Remember the publican's prayer (Luke 18:10–14)

       a. "God be merciful to me a sinner"

       b. "This man went down to his house justified"

    3. The great invitation to salvation is a call to receive mercy (Rom. 10:9–13)

    4. God's grace grants merit to sinners who request it

III. Conclusion

  A. *God's Mercy Is Extended to Those Who Don't Deserve It*

  B. *Are You Weak and Sinful Enough to Need Mercy?*

    1. "This weak one knew his own sins too well to think of merit or appeal to anything but the grace of God" (Spurgeon)

    2. God's grace makes weak ones stong

A Little Lower than the Angels

I. Introduction

    A. *This Is a Psalm of Praise and Passion*

        1. "How excellent is thy name in all the earth!"

        2. God is worthy of our highest praise

        3. "No heart can measure, no tongue can describe half the greatness of God" (Spurgeon)

    B. *All Creation Joins the Chorus of Adoration*

        1. "The heavens declare the glory of God" (Ps. 19:1)

        2. "Ascend to the highest heaven, or dive into the lowest hell, and God is both praised in everlasting song or justified in terrible vengeance" (Spurgeon)

    C. *What About Humans?*

II. Body

    A. *Compare Humans to the Rest of Creation (vv. 1–4)*

        1. How small we seem in relation to the universe!

           a. The vastness of creation makes us humble

           b. The intricacies of creation amaze us

        2. The grace of God in caring about us proves His love

           a. "What is man, that thou art mindful of him?"

           b. We do not deserve the attention of the Almighty

        3. Children are least likely to question God's love

           a. "Out of the mouths of babes"

           b. Salvation comes through childlike faith (Matt. 18:2)

    B. *Contrast Humans and Angels (vv. 5–8)*

        1. "For thou hast made him a little lower than the angels"

           a. Angels are universal messengers of God, doing His will

           b. People have earthly responsibilities to do God's will

        2. Man has been given dominion (authority) over the earth

   a.   We are lower than angels but higher than
        animals
   b.   We are to be good stewards of the earth and
        animals
   3.   How are we measuring up in our ruling roles?
        a.   Are we good representatives of our Creator,
             Redeemer
        b.   Does our conduct in all areas remind others of
             His love?
C.   *Jesus Condescended to Be Made Lower than Angels
     (Heb. 2:9)*
   1.   Here is the miracle of the Incarnation
        a.   The Creator of angels became lower than them
        b.   He humbled Himself to bring us salvation
   2.   Christ became the "Son of Man" to save man
        (Luke 19:10)
        a.   He who was above all things became lower
             than the angels
        b.   This even included death on the Cross to pay
             for our sins (Phil. 2:5–7)
   3.   Now Christ is exalted above the angels (Eph. 1:21–
        23)

III.   Conclusion
A.   *Men and Angels Will Bow at the Name of Jesus (Phil.
     2:10–11)*
B.   *"Jesus" Is the Only Name by Which We Can Be Saved*
   1.   What does the name of Jesus mean to you?
   2.   How excellent is that name in all the earth!

Ultimate Satisfaction

Series in Psalms   *Psalm 17:15*

I. **Introduction**
   A. *This Is a Psalm of Prayer, Protection, and Perfection*
      1. David says his prayer is sincere, his life clean
          (vv. 1–5)
      2. David asks to be protected from the wicked
          (vv. 6–14)
      3. David looks forward to meeting his Lord (v. 15)
   B. *This Is a Psalm That Looks Forward to Ultimate
       Satisfaction*
      1. Many desire and seek after things in this world that
          do not satisfy
          a. Riches and momentary thrills do not satisfy
          b. Personal success and acclaim do not satisfy
      2. Problems and dashed dreams may even keep the
          faithful from being satisfied
   C. *When Will We Find True Satisfaction?*

II. **Body**
   A. *We Will Be Satisfied When We See the Lord*
      1. "I will behold thy face in righteousness"
      2. This hope sustained David during severe trials
          a. It sustained him when the wicked oppressed
              him (v. 9)
          b. It sustained him when he was surrounded by
              deadly enemies (v. 9)
      3. In his afflictions, Job looked forward to seeing his
          Redeemer (Job 19:25–27)
          a. This hope encouraged him when he lost
              everything
          b. It gave him strength when condemned by his
              friends
      4. Do you have this blessed hope for the future?
   B. *We Will Be Satisfied When We Are Resurrected*
      1. "I shall be satisfied when I awake"
      2. David lived each day assured of his coming
          resurrection
          a. If his enemies killed him, he would rise again

119

        b.   If he was buried, he would come out of the grave

    3.   We can live daily with this same confidence

        a.   Our Lord arose and so shall we

        b.   Christ is the firstfruits of the coming Resurrection (1 Cor. 15:20)

    4.   The hope of resurrection removes death's sting (1 Cor. 15:55)

    5.   Our future victory over the grave gives present peace (1 Cor. 15:57)

C.   *We Will Be Satisfied When We Are Like Jesus*

    1.   "When I awake, with thy likeness"

    2.   When we rise we will be like Christ (1 John 3:1–3)

    3.   "My satisfaction is to come. I shall awake at the sound of the trumpet, wake to everlasting joy, because I will arise in Your likeness" (Spurgeon)

    4.   Anticipation of being like Jesus brings light to dark days

        a.   This purifying hope gives victory over temptation

        b.   It encourages all who feel they've failed again and again

III.   Conclusion

A.   *Are You Tired of Searching for Something to Satisfy?*

B.   *Come to Jesus and End Your Fruitless Quest*

    1.   Christ gives salvation, hope, and ultimate satisfaction

    2.   Accept His invitation and find the One who satisfies the soul (John 6:35)

The Teacher of Sinners

Series in Psalms   *Psalm 25:8*

I. Introduction
  A. *The Good News of Grace Is That God Loves Sinners*
    1. God is good: He cannot be blamed for the sinner's plight
    2. God is upright: He has provided a way of salvation
  B. *God Teaches Sinners the Way to Eternal Life*
    1. "What a ragged school for God to teach in!" (Spurgeon)
    2. God meets us where we are: lost in sin
    3. Through grace, God lifts us to where we ought to be
  C. *How Does God Teach Sinners?*

II. Body
  A. *God Teaches Sinners Through the Message of the Cross*
    1. Reconciliation to God is through the Cross (Eph. 2:16)
    2. God has proven His love to us at the Cross (Rom. 5:8)
    3. "Here the goodness and righteousness of God appear in friendly union. To see them united one must stand at the foot of the cross and view them blended in the sacrifice of the Lord Jesus" (Spurgeon)
    4. The Cross divides humanity into the saved and the lost (Luke 24:39–43)
      a. One thief trusted Christ and was pardoned
      b. One thief rejected Christ and perished
      c. On which side of the Cross are you?
  B. *God Teaches Sinners Through the Lives of Christians*
    1. We are to shine as lights in the world (Phil. 2:15)
    2. We are living epistles for all to read (2 Cor. 3:2)
      a. The responsibility of Christians is to be consistent
      b. Hypocrisy should have no place in our lives
      c. Others are watching; souls are at stake

        3.   Many have been saved because they saw Christ in others

        4.   Will sinners come to Jesus because of you and me?

   C. *God Teaches Sinners Through Circumstances in Their Lives*

        1.   Paul met Christ in a crisis on the road to Damascus (Acts 9)

           a.   He had been proud, self-centered, religious, and lost

           b.   An experience that brought him to the end of himself changed everything

           c.   Meeting Jesus in this crisis brought him salvation

        2.   The Philippian jailer believed because of an earthquake

           a.   He thought all the prisoners had escaped

           b.   The prisoners being present prompted his enduring question

           c.   "What must I do to be saved?" (Acts 16:30)

        3.   What circumstance has caused you to see your need of Christ?

        4.   This experience has come your way to bring you to Jesus

III. Conclusion

   A. *God Is Reaching Out to You*

   B. *Jesus Is Showing You the Way*

   C. *Respond to His Love and Be Saved Today*

The Defeat of Fear

Series in Psalms   *Psalm 27:1*

I. Introduction

    A. Fear Stalks Us All

    B. Fear Was the First Evidence of the Fall (Gen. 3:10)

        1. Adam and Eve went into hiding

        2. Adam's response to God's call was, "I was afraid"

    B. This Is a Psalm to Drive Our Fears Away

        1. This psalm can give us light for darkness

        2. This psalm can give us salvation for condemnation

        3. This psalm can give us strength for weakness

II. Body

    A. This Psalm Declares a Light for Darkness

        1. "The LORD is my light"

        2. God's purpose is to bring light out of darkness

            a. This was true in Creation (Gen. 1:1–4)

            b. This was true in the Incarnation (John 1:1–9)

            c. This is true in our lives at salvation (John 8:12)

        3. "Salvation finds us in the dark, but it does not leave us there; it gives light to those who sit in the valley of the shadow of death" (Spurgeon)

        4. This is our great transition from darkness to light (Col. 1:12–13)

            a. We are delivered from the power of darkness

            b. We are translated into the kingdom of Christ

    B. This Psalm Declares Salvation for Condemnation

        1. "The LORD is my light *and my salvation*"

        2. We are all sinners, all condemned (Rom. 3:10–23; John 3:17–19)

            a. Our condemnation doesn't require even one more sin

            b. We are already condemned by our unbelief

        3. Christ delivers us from condemnation (John 3:17)

            a. We do not have to do good works to be loved by Him

            b. We are saved by grace through faith apart from works (Eph. 2:8–9)

      4.   Here are two great words for believers: "no condemnation" (Rom. 8:1)

   C. *This Psalm Declares Strength for Weakness*

      1.   "The LORD is the strength of my life"

      2.   Christ changes our eternal destination and our daily lives

         a.   He gives strength for every task (Phil. 4:13)

         b.   He gives strength when we are weary (Isa. 40:28–31)

         c.   He gives strength when we're fearful (Ps. 27:1, 14)

      3.   "Our life derives all its strength from Him who is the author of it" (Spurgeon)

      4.   Here are two great promises of strength

         a.   "The joy of the LORD is your strength" (Neh. 8:10)

         b.   "In quietness and confidence shall be your strength" (Isa. 30:15)

III.   Conclusion

   A. *Do You Fear the Power of Darkness? Come to Jesus, the Light*

   B. *Do You Feel Condemned? Come to Jesus for Salvation*

   C. *Do You Feel Weak? Come to Jesus and Get Strength for the Day*

Try God

Psalm 34:1–8

I. Introduction

A. *There Are Many Challenges in Life*
  1. Here is a challenge from David, a man who has found God faithful
  2. Here is a challenge from a man with a heart filled with praise

B. *David Challenges Everyone to Try God*
  1. "O taste and see that the LORD is good"
  2. Blessings are promised to those who accept this challenge

C. *Why Did David Issue This Challenge?*

II. Body

A. *The Lord Had Delivered Him from His Fears (v. 4)*
  1. "He heard me, and delivered me from all my fears"
    a. When afraid, David prayed ("I sought the LORD")
    b. Answered prayer made David a praising person
  2. David had many reasons to fear
    a. He tended sheep alone in his youth (1 Sam. 17:34)
    b. He faced mighty Goliath (1 Sam. 17:39–58)
  3. David sought the Lord when he was afraid
    a. David is a good example for us all
    b. The "peace be still" of Jesus calms our fears
  4. God is bigger than our fears
  5. Why should we ever be afraid? (Ps. 27:1)

B. *The Lord Had Saved Him Out of All His Troubles (v. 6)*
  1. "This poor man cried, and the LORD heard him"
    a. Sometimes all we can do is cry out to God
    b. These are fearful but faith-building times
  2. Man's extremity often becomes God's opportunity
    a. This is true at salvation
    b. Unable to save ourselves, we cry out to Jesus
    c. He saves us when we cannot save ourselves
  3. David found his Lord was up to the occasion

       a.   God saved him "out of all his troubles"
           (complete deliverance)
       b.   He can do the same for you and me

  C. *The Lord Had Delivered Him in Times of Danger (v. 7)*
    1. David discovered he was not alone
       a.   Even in times of peril he could feel secure
       b.   God's deliverance of His people is found
           throughout the Bible
    2. When pursued by angry Saul, David had been
       delivered
    3. When surrounded by his enemies, he was protected
    4. No wonder he issued his enduring challenge

III.   Conclusion
  A. *O Taste and See That the Lord Is Good*
    1. "Faith is the soul's taste" (Spurgeon)
    2. Those who come to Christ find Him good
  B. *Accept David's Challenge and Try God Today*

Stop That Sinful Worrying

Series in Psalms   *Psalm 37:1–7*

I. Introduction
   A. *Worry Is the Worthless Emotion*
      1. Worry doesn't help solve tomorrow's problems
      2. It drains strength needed to face today's difficulties
      3. The psalmist calls us to stop worrying (Fret not)
   B. *This Psalm Helps with a Problem Common to All*
      1. "A psalm in which the Lord sweetly quiets the common complaints of His people" (Spurgeon)
      2. David was fretting over the prosperity of the wicked
      3. What's your common complaint? What makes you a worrier?
   C. *Four Words Will Enable Us to Win over Worry*

II. Body
   A. *The First Word Is Trust (v. 3)*
      1. Trust is another word for faith
         a. The Christian life begins in faith (Eph. 2:8–9; Rom. 5:1; Acts 16:31)
         b. Without faith it is impossible to please God (Heb. 11:6)
      2. Christians are to live by faith (Rom. 1:17)
      3. The peace of God comes through faith (Phil. 4:6–8)
         a. Fear (worry) is the opposite of faith
         b. Faith drives our fears away
      4. "Faith cures fretting" (Spurgeon)
   B. *The Second Word Is Delight (v. 4)*
      1. To delight is to take great pleasure
         a. We are to take great pleasure in the Lord
         b. Our walk with Him is to be our delight
      2. What gives us pleasure reveals the reality of our faith
         a. If money is our delight, we will fret at the thought of losing it
         b. If success is our delight, we will fret at the thought of failure

  3. When Christ is our delight, we will find pleasure in reading His Word and in prayer
C. *The Third Word Is Commit (v. 5)*
  1. To commit is to entrust something to another person
    a. We are to entrust our way to the Lord
    b. We are to give Him our trials and treasures, our todays and tomorrows
  2. At salvation, we entrust our souls to Christ
  3. We can then safely entrust the future to Him
D. *The Fourth Word Is Rest (v. 5)*
  1. To rest is to relax completely
  2. Christians are to relax in the love and care of Christ
    a. Why then are there so many anxious Christians?
    b. How can we fret when the future is in His loving hands?
  3. Resting in Jesus brings peace in daily life

III. Conclusion
A. *Four Words Can Change Worriers into Winners*
B. *What Part Do These Four Words Play in Your Life?*

When Silence Is Golden

Series in Psalms   *Psalm 39:1*

I. Introduction

A. *The Psalmist Makes a Good Resolution*
   1. It is a resolution about sinful words
   2. It is a resolution that would be good for us all
   3. "It is good when we can strengthen ourselves in doing right by remembering a wise resolution" (Spurgeon)

B. *There Are Times When It Is Better to Refrain from Speaking*
   1. At times silence is golden
   2. The Holy Spirit gives self-control, which includes tongue control (Gal. 5:22–23)

C. *Here Are Some Examples and Exhortations About Silence*

II. Body

A. *Here, David Is the Silent Psalmist (v. 1)*
   1. "I will keep my mouth with a bridle"
      a. David was determined to control his tongue
      b. He saw this as evidence of divine discipline
   2. James emphasized this same truth (James 3)
      a. Both David and James spoke of bridling the tongue
      b. Both saw this as a mark of true faith
   3. Consider David's secrets of sanctified silence
      a. He made a determined commitment: "My mouth shall not transgress" (Ps. 17:3)
      b. He uttered a sincere prayer: "Set a watch, O LORD, before my mouth" (Ps. 141:3)

B. *Here Are Some Situations That Call for Silence (v. 1)*
   1. "While the wicked is before me"
      a. Some people are listening for loose lips
      b. Some want juicy gossip to pass along
      c. Some want to find hypocrisy in our words
   2. At times silence is better than speaking
      a. Keep silent when tempted to criticize

   b. Keep silent when the sins of others are being
       discussed
   c. Keep silent when among chronic complainers
   d. Keep silent when people are grumbling about
       church leaders
   e. Keep silent when speaking may ruin a
       reputation
   f. Keep silent when anger would cause words to
       be harsh
 3. Never allow words to harm the work of Christ
C. *Christ Is the Silent Savior (Isa. 53:7)*
 1. Jesus was silent before His accusers
     a. He was silent before Herod and Pilate
     b. He was silent before those who cursed Him
 2. Consider what Peter said about his silent Savior
     (1 Peter 2:20–24)
     a. "When he was reviled, reviled not again"
     b. "When he suffered, he threatened not"

III. Conclusion
A. *David Uttered a Great Prayer for a Pure Heart and
   Tongue (Ps. 19:14)*
B. *Our Hearts Can Be Right with God; Our Words Can
   Please Him*

From the Pit to the Pinnacle of Praise

Series in Psalms *Psalm 40:1–3*

I. **Introduction**
   A. *Can We Be Patient in a Pit?*
      1. We all go through trials—even Christians
      2. In trouble, the psalmist cried out to God for help
         a. The answer was slow in coming
         b. Faith enabled him to remain patient until help arrived
   B. *Jesus Is the Supreme Example of Patience Under Pressure*
      1. He was patient in Gethsemane, when on trial, even on the Cross
      2. "Job in the ash pit does not equal Jesus on the cross" (Spurgeon)
   C. *Lessons Are to Be Gained from the Pit to the Pinnacle of Praise*

II. **Body**
   A. *When We're Sinking, God Is Seeking (vv. 1–2)*
      1. We can be sure God is aware of our need
         a. Nothing escapes God's view nor takes Him by surprise
         b. We may think He doesn't care, but He is there
      2. Jesus came to seek and save the lost (Luke 19:10)
      3. The Shepherd seeks His wandering sheep (Luke 15:4)
      4. Our Lord knows about the pit of miry clay
         a. He awaits the call of all sinking ones
         b. He will answer and lift them up . . . right on time
      5. God sets our feet on the solid Rock and brings purpose to our lives
   B. *When We've Been Saved, God Gives a Song (vv. 2–3)*
      1. "And he hath put a new song in my mouth"
         a. It is not a sorrowful song
         b. It is a song of praise
      2. It is praise for answered prayer

131

3. It is praise for being lifted out of the horrible pit
4. It is praise for escaping the miry clay
5. It is praise for being set on the solid Rock
6. It is praise for a new life built on the promises of God

C. *When We Start Praising, People Start Praying (v. 3)*
   1. Praising saints make praying sinners
      a. Praise proves the reality of our faith
      b. Praise demonstrates the power of God's love and grace
   2. "Many shall see it and fear and shall trust in the Lord"
      a. Those in pits of miry clay long to be lifted to safety
      b. They want something solid on which to build their lives
      c. They long to place their feet on the solid Rock
   3. Pouting Christians are poor representatives of their Lord
   4. Praising Christians are missionaries wherever they go

III. Conclusion
A. *Have You Been Lifted from the Pit of Sin?*
B. *Has Jesus Filled Your Heart with Songs of Joy?*
C. *Prepare to Welcome Others into the Fellowship of Praise*

Thirsting for God

Series in Psalms *Psalm 42:1–2*

I. Introduction

   A. *This Psalm Meets Us Where We Are*
1. We all know the urgency of thirst
2. We can live longer without food than without water
3. We all know the satisfaction of a drink of cold water when we're thirsty

   B. *The Psalmist Links Physical and Spiritual Thirst*
1. This thirsty one concludes that only God can quench his thirsty soul
2. "Give David his God and he is as content as a thirsty deer which finally, after a long search, quenches his thirst and is perfectly happy" (Spurgeon)

   C. *Here Are Some Thoughts About Thirsty People*

II. Body

   A. *A Thirsty Woman Was at a Well (John 4:5–15)*
1. Jesus met a woman of Samaria at a well
   a. She had a story to tell
   b. Life hadn't treated her well
2. Her inner thirst was revealed in her failed marriages
   a. She kept looking for a man to bring satisfaction
   b. She had been married five times and was now living with one not her husband
3. Jesus knew all about her thirst
   a. He knows all about your fruitless search for happiness and peace of mind
   b. He offers living water to quench your inner thirst and end your search

   B. *A Thirsty Man Was in Hell (Luke 16:19–24)*
1. A man tried to quench his thirst with wealth
   a. Financially, he was doing very well, living lavishly every day
   b. He was so unlike the poor sickly beggar at his gate

133

  2. Then something went wrong for the rich man: he lost his health
   a. When the rich man died, his thirst lived on
   b. This may be one of the severest torments of hell
   c. He begged the beggar to bring a drop of water for his tortured tongue
  3. Jesus endured the thirst of hell on the Cross
   a. "I thirst," He cried before He died
   b. Christ died that we might never thirst again
   c. He bore our hell on Calvary so we can go to heaven

C. *An Invitation God Wants Us to Tell (Rev. 22:17)*
  1. "Let him that is athirst come"
  2. Thirsty ones are invited to take of the water of life
  3. This living water is free for the taking . . . by faith
  4. At the Cross, blood and water flowed from Jesus' side
   a. Blood announced forgiveness of sins
   b. Water announced a fountain for thirsty souls

III. Conclusion

A. *Are You Thirsty?*
B. *Come in Faith to the One Who Offers Living Water*
C. *Come and Never Thirst Again*

When to Talk to Ourselves About God

Psalm 42:5

I. **Introduction**
   A. *The Psalms Play on All the Strings of Our Emotions*
      1. They meet us in despair when all hope seems gone
      2. They lift us on wings of praise, giving songs in the night
   B. *This Text Finds the Psalmist Talking to Himself*
      1. "As though he were two men, the psalmist talks to himself. His faith reasons with his fears, his hope argues with his sorrows" (Spurgeon)
      2. This text appears three times in the Psalms (42:5, 11; 43:5)
   C. *Self-Talk May Be Just What We Need*

II. **Body**
   A. *We May Need Self-Talk When We Are Discouraged*
      1. "Why art thou cast down, O my soul?"
      2. We all go through times of discouragement
         a. Poor health robs us of strength
         b. Income is low and debts are high
         c. Dreams are dashed and castles tumble
         d. Family and friends disappoint us
      3. "David scolds David out of the dumps" (Spurgeon)
      4. What are we doing living under the circumstances?
         a. Have we forgotten the promises of God? (Rom. 8:28)
         b. Have we been doubting God's love? (Rom. 8:38–39)
   B. *We May Need Self-Talk When We Are Upset*
      1. "Why art thou disquieted within me?"
      2. We respond faithlessly when upset
         a. Jacob thought all was against him (Gen. 42:36)
         b. Elijah wanted to die (1 Kings 19:4)
         c. Job wished he hadn't been born (Job 3:1–13)
         d. The disciples panicked in a storm (Mark 4:38)
      3. Distress should remind us that God's grace is sufficient
         a. Paul found God's grace to be enough (2 Cor. 12:9)

135

      b. "Grace swims to our aid though the waves roar and be troubled" (Spurgeon)

C. *We May Need Self-Talk to Be Reminded of God's Faithfulness*
1. "Hope thou in God"
   a. "Hope carries stars in her eyes" (Spurgeon)
   b. Going through trouble develops hope (Rom. 5:1–5)
2. Our hope rests in the faithful One
3. This is a text of hope in a time of tears (Lam. 3:21–26)
   a. God's mercies are new every morning
   b. "Great is thy faithfulness"
4. God is always up to the occasion

III. Conclusion
A. *Let's Talk to Ourselves About God's Grace*
B. *Let's Talk to Ourselves About God's Goodness*
C. *Let's Talk to Jesus About Trading Our Fears for Faith*

Breaking the Grip of the Grave

Series in Psalms   *Psalm 49:6–20*

I. Introduction

   A. *Life's Greatest Deception Started in Eden*

      1. Satan said, "Ye shall not surely die" (Gen. 3:4)

      2. Millions live as if this lie were true

      3. They store up riches as if they would never leave them

   B. *Sin Has Brought the Prospect of Death to Us All (Heb. 9:27)*

      1. Graves await the rich and the poor

         a. Funeral processions and cemeteries preach this message

         b. We each have an appointment with the grave

      2. How do we prepare for that coming day?

II. Body

   A. *We Cannot Prepare Through Increased Education (vv. 6–14)*

      1. "Wise men die, likewise the fool and the brutish person perish"

      2. Degrees cannot deliver us from death

      3. Learned people have been unable to find a way to escape life's common end

         a. Eternal life cannot be gained by accumulating facts on healthy living

         b. Even the wisest have been unable to avoid the grip of the grave

      3. Medical science comes up empty in its search for a pill to give eternal life

         a. Miracle drugs work only for a season

         b. Diseases have been conquered, but life still ultimately ends

      4. In spite of earthly honors, we all march steadily toward the grave

   B. *We Cannot Prepare Through Increased Wealth (vv. 16–20)*

      1. "Be not afraid when one is made rich"

         a. Expensive homes do not increase the length of life

137

           b.   Earthly honor and glory fade; they cannot prevent death

    2.   Wealth is worthless in the grave

           a.   We can't take wealth with us

           b.   Present pomp perishes with life's last breath

    3.   "All must pass through the river of death naked. Not a rag of clothing, not a coin of treasure, not a bit of honor can the dying person carry with him" (Spurgeon)

    4.   The grave levels the ground between the haves and have nots

           a.   The rich man and Lazarus both died (Luke 16:19–31)

           b.   Let us not fret over those who gain earth's temporary trinkets (Ps. 37:1)

C.   *We Can Only Prepare for the Grave Through Faith in Christ (v. 15)*

    1.   "God will redeem my soul from the power of the grave"

    2.   Job knew his Redeemer would provide victory over the grave (Job 19:25)

    3.   Jesus demonstrated His power over the grave

           a.   He resurrected Lazarus and others (John 11)

           b.   He came out of the grave alive after the Crucifixion (Luke 24)

    4.   The living Christ saves all who come to Him, giving them eternal life (Heb. 7:25)

III.   Conclusion

A.   *We Should All Be Prepared for the Day of Death (Amos 4:12)*

B.   *We're Not Prepared to Live Until We're Prepared to Die*

C.   *Are You Prepared to Escape the Grip of the Grave?*

What God Wants Us to Know

Series in Psalms Ends   *Psalm 50:1–15*

I. Introduction

A. *This Psalm Reminds Us of God's Power and Grace (v. 1)*

   1. "Jehovah's dominion extends over the whole earth. The east and the west are called to hear the God who makes His sun rise on every quarter of the globe" (Spurgeon)

   2. This psalm ought to fill our hearts with praise (v. 23)

B. *This Psalm Is for the People of God (vv. 2–5)*

   1. "Gather my saints together unto me"

   2. Here's what God wants His people to know about Him

II. Body

A. *God Wants Us to Know About His Righteousness (vv. 5–6)*

   1. God always does right

      a. Some question this when things go wrong

      b. But we can be sure that God always acts in righteousness

   2. God is good . . . all the time

   3. God's righteousness was demonstrated at the Cross

      a. We are all sinners bound for hell (Rom. 3:10–23)

      b. God's love called for salvation but His justice had to be satisfied

      c. God's righteousness provided a way

         (1) At the Cross, God was just and the justifier of sinners

         (2) The blood of Christ paid for our sins

   4. God's righteousness is the joy of heaven (Rev. 19:1–2)

B. *God Wants Us to Know About His Resources (vv. 9–12)*

   1. "Every beast of the forest is mine, and the cattle upon a thousand hills"

   2. Our Lord owns everything

        a.   "How could Israel imagine that the most High God, possessor of heaven and earth, had need of beasts for offerings when all the countless herds and flocks that find shelter in a thousand forests and wildernesses belong to Him? Not only the wild animals but also the tamer creatures were all His own" (Spurgeon)

        b.   Paul said, "But my God shall supply all your need according to his riches in glory by Christ Jesus" (Phil. 4:19)

    3.   Why then do we worry about how God will meet our needs?

    4.   The one who feeds the birds and clothes the flowers will care for us (Matt. 6:26–31)

C. *God Wants Us to Know About His Response to Our Call (v. 15)*

    1.   Here is a double promise for times of trouble
        a.   "Call upon me in the day of trouble"
        b.   "I will deliver thee, and thou shalt glorify me"

    2.   The disciples found this true in a storm on the Sea of Galilee (Mark 4:36–41)

    3.   Jeremiah found this true at a difficult time in his life (Jer. 33:3)

    4.   The thief on the cross found this true and received paradise (Luke 23:43)

III. Conclusion

A. *Have You Been Wondering If God Will Do Right?*

B. *Have You Been Worried About Meeting Some Pressing Need?*

C. *Call Out to God and Find Him Sufficient for You Today*

Why Remember?

1 Corinthians 11:25–26

I. Introduction
  A. *Communion Is a Time to Remember Again*
      1. This bread will remind us of Christ's broken body
      2. This cup will remind us of Christ's blood shed on the Cross
  B. *Christians Repeatedly Return to the Memorial Table*
      1. Some return weekly, some monthly, some quarterly, some annually
      2. As often as we return, we are to remember (v. 25)
      3. Why do we keep returning to remember?

II. Body
  A. *Remembering Reminds Us of Redemption (vv. 24–25)*
      1. These symbols of Christ's death tell the story of redemption
      2. Great hymns give tune and voice to this wonderful story of love
          a. "I will sing of my Redeemer"
          b. "Love found a way to redeem my soul"
          c. "Redeemed, how I love to proclaim it"
      3. To redeem is to buy back things or persons previously sold
      4. We had been sold in the slave market of sin (in Eden and in our lives)
      5. Jesus died to buy us back, to set us free, to redeem us
          a. Remember the suffering Savior purchasing our pardon
          b. Remember the price He paid (1 Peter 1:17)
          c. Hear the Savior's cry of complete redemption: "It is finished"
  B. *Remembering Reminds Us of the Resurrection (v. 26)*
      1. The Resurrection proves the deity of Christ (John 2:19–20)
      2. Three great guarantees are in the Resurrection
          a. The guarantee is of our Savior (Rom. 1:4)

        b.   The guarantee is of our salvation (1 Cor. 15:14–20)

        c.   The guarantee is of our similar resurrection (1 Cor. 15:20–23)

   3.   There would be no continuing Communion without the Resurrection

   4.   There would be no church without the Resurrection

   5.   There would be no hope of heaven without the Resurrection

   6.   Let this Communion remind us that we trust and serve a living Savior

  C. *Remembering Reminds Us of Christ's Return (v. 26)*

   1.   We observe Communion "till he come"

   2.   Each Communion service is prophetic

        a.   The words of the prophets ought to thrill our souls

        b.   This One whose death we remember is coming again

   3.   Remembering the prophetic significance of Communion should fill us with expectation

        a.   Every Communion service is part of the countdown to His coming

        b.   The hope of Christ's return purifies us; it prepares us for Communion (1 John 3:3)

III.   **Conclusion**

  A. *What Will This Communion Do for You?*

   1.   Will remembering cause you to live in the light of the Cross?

   2.   Will remembering move you to prepare for Christ's return?

  B. *Will You Look Forward to the Next Time We Meet to Remember?*

The Sermon I Would Preach on Sunday
If I Knew I Would Die on Monday

Psalm 90:12

I. **Introduction**
   A. *Richard Baxter Had a Goal in His Preaching*
      1. He wanted to preach as if he'd never preach again and as a dying man to dying people
      2. I want to preach to you today with the urgency of Baxter's goal
   B. *The Psalmist Calls Us to Number Our Days*
      1. This is good advice for us all
      2. Preachers die too and should be aware of life's brevity
   C. *What I Would Say If This Was My Last Sermon*

II. **Body**
   A. *The First Part of My Sermon Would Be to Those I Love*
      1. We all have responsibilities to those closest to us
         a. I would assure my family of my faith in Christ, which gives me eternal life
         b. Many leave loved ones wondering whether they will see them again
      2. I would tell them of the time I trusted Christ as my Savior
         a. I would describe the times God spoke to my heart about His love
         b. I would give thanks for those who lived the Christian life before me
         c. I would describe the church service when I opened my heart to Jesus (Rev. 3:20)
            (1) I would recall the words of the pastor at the invitation
            (2) I would take my loved ones into the miracle of that moment
      3. I would share Bible verses that gave assurance of my salvation (John 6:37; 1 John 5:11–13)
   B. *The Second Part of My Sermon Would Be to Show Where I'll Live*
      1. When I die I'll move to a new address: heaven

       a.   At death, Christians depart from earth (John 13:1; John 16:7; 2 Tim.4:6)

       b.   We move to a better place (Phil. 1:21–23)

       c.   We immediately leave our bodies and move to heaven (2 Cor. 5:8)

  2.   Jesus has been preparing a place there for me (John 14:1–3)

  3.   Let me tell you about this place to which I'm moving

       a.   Heaven is a place of music (Rev. 5:9)

       b.   Heaven is a place of rest (Rev. 14:13)

       c.   Heaven is a place of rejoicing (Rev. 19:7)

       d.   Heaven is a place of beauty (Rev. 21:10–23)

  4.   Tomorrow I'll be living in a better place

C.   *The Third Part of My Sermon Would Be an Appeal to the Lost*

  1.   Jesus came to seek and save the lost (Luke 19:10)

  2.   My last sermon would be an urgent appeal to my hearers to be saved

       a.   I would preach sin as deadly and damning

       b.   I would preach the love of Christ as warm and wonderful

       c.   I would preach the Cross as full payment for our sins

  3.   My last invitation would be long, tearful, and pleading—my final call

III. Conclusion

A.   *We Are Not Guaranteed Life Will Last Until Tomorrow*

B.   *Today Is the Day of Salvation (2 Cor. 6:2)*

C.   *Come to Jesus for Salvation Today!*

Peter's Call to Holy Living

1 Peter 1:15–25

I. Introduction
A. *Get to Know Peter*
   1. Peter journeyed from defeat to victory
      a. He journeyed from denying his Lord to declaring the gospel
      b. He journeyed from pride to pointing others to Christ
      c. He journeyed from an explosive temper to walking as Jesus walked
   2. To know Peter well is to know ourselves well
   3. Peter's struggles and successes are much like our own
B. *This Epistle Begins with Praise (vv. 3–5)*
   1. Peter had personal experience with "abundant mercy"
   2. He learned to look beyond his trials to triumph
C. *Why Does Peter Call Us to Holy Living?*

II. Body
A. *God Is Holy (v. 15)*
   1. "He which hath called you is holy"
   2. God's holiness is declared throughout the Bible
      a. Moses learned that God is holy (Exod. 3:1–6)
      b. Isaiah learned that God is holy (Isa. 6:1–8)
      c. John learned that God is holy (Rev. 4:8)
   3. God's holiness is unchanging; He is unmoved by shifting moral standards
   4. We will someday stand before this Holy One to give an account of ourselves (Rom. 14:12)
B. *The Goal Is Holy Living (v. 16)*
   1. "Be ye holy; for I am holy"
   2. Mistaken goals are success, wealth, public praise
      a. Goals based on earthly gain will disappoint us
      b. Holy living brings eternal rewards
   3. Holy living identifies us as the children of God
      a. We are to present our bodies as holy, living, sacrifices to God (Rom. 12:1)

145

  b. This kind of commitment reveals God's will for our lives (Rom. 12:2)

 4. Peter tells us to see Jesus as our example of holy living (1 Peter 2:21–25)

  a. Jesus suffered without responding in kind

  b. Jesus was reviled but refused to react in anger

  c. We are to follow His steps

C. *Grace Bridges the Gap (vv. 17–25)*

 1. Focusing on God's holiness brings conviction of sin

  a. God is holy and we are not; this could bring despair

  b. What can we do to bridge the gap between us and God

 2. We cannot bridge the gap through good works (Isa. 64:6)

 3. We cannot bridge the gap through religious ceremonies

 4. Grace bridges the gap between sinners and our holy God

III. Conclusion

A. *Holy Living Cannot Be Achieved Through Human Effort*

B. *Holy Living Is Produced by the Holy Spirit Living Within*

C. *The Holy Spirit Brings Holiness in Those Yielded to Him (Gal. 5:22–23)*

Living Stones

I. Introduction

A. *Two Key Questions Were Asked in Peter's Life*
   1. "Whom do men say that I am?" (Matt. 16:15–18)
   2. "Lovest thou me more than these?" (John 21:15–17)

B. *Consider the First of These Questions*
   1. What was the impact of this question on Peter's life?
   2. What has been the impact of this question on Christianity?
   3. How did Peter understand the Lord's response to his answer?

C. *Stones and Certainties*

II. Body

A. *Peter Was the Stone (Matt. 16:13–20)*
   1. The retreat at Caesarea Phillipi was a resting and learning time for the disciples
   2. The Lord asked, "Whom do men say that I am?"
   3. Peter answered, "Thou art the Christ, the Son of the living God'"
   4. Consider the Lord's response and the confusion concerning it
      a. "Thou art Peter, and upon this rock I will build my church"
      b. Some think Christ was saying Peter was the rock on which He would build His church
      c. Peter understood this to mean he was a stone in the church built on Christ the Rock
      d. "There is in the Greek a play upon words [*Petros*—literally, 'a little rock']. He does not promise to build His church on Peter but upon Himself, as Peter himself is careful to tell us (1 Peter 2:4–9)" (Scofield)

B. *Christians Are Living Stones (1 Peter 2:4)*
1. Peter calls all believers stones, just as he was called a stone by Jesus
2. Why stones?
    a. Nothing is more dead than a stone; they are cold and unresponsive
    c. This describes all people without Christ (Rom. 6:23)
3. But believers are stones come to life—"living stones" (Eph. 2:5)
    a. This declares the power of Christ to give life
    b. The most desperate and sinful can be saved (Col. 2:13–14)
4. Living stones demonstrate variety in the church
    a. The church is not built of blocks but stones; no two stones are exactly alike
    b. Jesus will use each of us in a special way (Rom. 12; 1 Cor. 12–14)

C. *Jesus Christ Is the Cornerstone (1 Peter 2:4, 6–8)*
1. Christ is the chief cornerstone, the only foundation on which to build our lives
    a. All who do not build upon Him build on sand (Matt. 7:24–27)
    b. "Other foundation can no man lay" (1 Cor. 3:11)
2. This foundation is strong because it is solid rock
    a. "He is the Rock, his work is perfect" (Deut. 32:1–4)
    b. "The LORD is my rock and my fortress" (Ps. 18:2)
3. This Rock has been rejected by men (2:7; John 1:11–12)
4. Will you reject Christ, too, or build your life upon Him?

III. **Conclusion**
A. *We Are Transformed from Stones to Servants of the Living God (v. 9)*
B. *We Are to Be Living Examples of His Mercy to Sinners (v. 10)*

Quieting Our Critics

1 Peter 2:11–15

I. Introduction

A. *Peter Had Tender Love for Other Christians*
1. "Dearly beloved" signals his love for those to whom he writes
2. We need this kind of love between believers today

B. *Peter Had Common Ground with Sufferers for Christ*
1. "I beseech you as strangers and pilgrims" is a greeting of understanding
2. He knows the world is at odds with those who live for Christ

C. *How Do We Silence Those Who Persecute with Words?*

II. Body

A. *Be Clean (v. 11)*
1. "Abstain from fleshly lusts which war against the soul"
2. This is a war in which all believers find themselves
   a. It is as old as sin and as up-to-date as today's temptations
   b. Battlegrounds include the lust of the flesh, the lust of the eyes, the pride of life (1 John 2:16)
3. There have been many casualties in this battle
   a. Samson succumbed to the deceit of Delilah
   b. David succumbed while on his roof watching Bathsheba bathe
4. There have also been some great victories
   a. Joseph refused to yield to the advances of Potiphar's wife (Gen. 39)
   b. Jesus defeated Satan when tempted (Matt. 4; Heb. 4:15)
5. God has made provision for us to win every time (1 Cor. 10:13)

B. *Be Careful (v. 12)*
1. There are many critical spectators in this war
   a. Others are watching to see if our faith is real

149

        b. Many are hoping we will be defeated so they can criticize

    2. Our lives are being continually inspected by unbelievers

        a. We are to welcome this inspection, knowing our lives can stand the test

        b. Critical onlookers provide opportunities to prove our faith is genuine

    3. Why must we be so careful to be absolutely honest and moral?

        a. We represent Jesus Christ to the world (2 Cor. 5:20)

        b. We are to shine as lights in a dark place (Phil. 2:15–16)

        c. Our light will glorify our Father in heaven (Matt. 5:16)

    4. If we care for Christ and souls, we will be careful

C. *Be Consistent (vv. 13–15)*

    1. Peter calls for more than Sunday-go-to-meeting Christianity

    2. The Christian message encompasses every area of life

        a. We have the unique privilege of being citizens of heaven (Phil. 3:20)

        b. We are also citizens of earth and are called to demonstrate we are different

        c. We are to submit ourselves to laws of the land, obeying them for the Lord's sake

    3. Living above reproach will impact our world for Christ

III. Conclusion

A. *We Silence Our Critics Through Clean, Careful, Consistent Living*

B. *We "Put to Silence the Ignorance of Foolish Men"*

C. *We May Also Influence Many of Them to Trust Our Lord*

Serving the Chief Shepherd

1 Peter 5:1–4

I. **Introduction**
  A. *Peter Had Advice to Church Leaders*
    1. He takes his place as one of them: "who am also an elder"
    2. He gives his credentials: a witness of Christ's suffering and a partaker of His glory
  B. *There Are Right Attitudes and Incentives for Feeding and Leading (vv. 2–3)*
    1. We do so not because we're forced into it but willingly
    2. We do so not to gain money but with eager desire to serve
    3. We do so not to lord it over people but to be examples to them

II. **Body**
  A. *Peter Looked upon the Lord as His Chief Shepherd*
    1. David had called the Lord his Shepherd; the one who cares for the sheep (Ps. 23)
    2. Jesus spoke of Himself as the Good Shepherd (John 10:11)
      a. He gave His life for the sheep, what an example for leaders!
      b. He was unlike the hireling; He didn't serve for personal gain
    3. The writer of Hebrews called Jesus the Great Shepherd (Heb. 13:20)
      a. He arose from the grave
      b. He is perfecting His people
    4. Peter called the Lord his Chief Shepherd
      a. He directs all earthly shepherds
      b. He gives direction to all leaders through His Word
      c. To Him we all must give an account
  B. *Peter Looked for the Return of the Chief Shepherd*
    1. "When the chief Shepherd shall appear"
    2. Peter had heard Jesus speak many times of His return

  a. He heard Jesus speak of going away and returning (John 14:1–3)

  b. He heard Jesus preach about the signs of His return (Matt. 24)

  c. At the Ascension Peter heard angels promise Christ's return (Acts 1:10–11)

 3. Peter's second epistle would major on the message of Christ's return

  a. He would warn of the scoffers to come, casting doubt on Christ's return (2 Peter 3:3)

  b. He would plead for holy living in light of Christ's return (2 Peter 3:10–11)

 4. Are you ready for Christ's return?

C. *Peter Looked Forward to Rewards Given by the Chief Shepherd*

 1. Consider Peter's claim to authority for what he is saying

  a. He had been with Jesus and was a witness of His suffering (v. 1)

  b. He had been at the Transfiguration as a witness of His glory (v. 1)

 2. He had witnessed the power of the Resurrection

  a. The Cross had seemed to end everything

  b. The Resurrection proved Christ would always keep His promises

 3. Jesus has promised to return and reward those who serve Him (Rev. 22:12)

III. Conclusion

A. *Do You Know the Chief Shepherd?*

B. *Are You Serving the Chief Shepherd?*

 1. Is doing His will your chief desire?

 2. Are you ready for His return to reward your service?

Getting Bad People Cleaned Up for Heaven

1 Corinthians 6:9–11

I. **Introduction**
  A. *The Gospel Is for Sinners*
    1. Corinth was a great place to reach sinners
    2. It was a city where lust was king and immorality common
  B. *The Gospel Changes Sinners*
    1. The gospel meets us where we are (1 Cor. 15:3–4)
    2. The gospel transforms us into what we ought to be (2 Cor. 5:17)
  C. *The Past, Present, and Future of Every Christian Is the Same*

II. **Body**
  A. *Consider the Way We Were*
    1. "The unrighteous shall not inherit the kingdom of God"
    2. Paul offered an unsavory list of sinners
      a. It was a list of immoral people
      b. It was a list of dishonest and unruly people
      c. Not one on Paul's list was fit for heaven
    3. "And such were some of you"
      a. Heaven-bound Christians were once hell-bound sinners
      b. This proves we are all lost until God saves us (Rom. 3:10–23)
    4. What changes the destination of these lost ones?
      a. God's grace rescues sinners and changes them
      b. In receiving Christ we become fit for heaven
  B. *Consider the Way We Are*
    1. We are washed
      a. We are made clean by the blood of Christ (Rev. 1:5)
      b. We are washed by the water of the Word (Eph. 5:26)
    2. We are sanctified: set apart for divine service
      a. God has a purpose for the life of each cleansed sinner (Rom. 5:1–8)

        b.   Even trials contribute to His purpose for our lives (Rom. 8:28–29)

    3. We are justified, declared righteous

        a.   This is possible because of Christ's finished work on the Cross (Rom. 3:25)

        b.   God is just and the justifier of those who believe (Rom. 3:26)

        c.   Our justification is not by works but by grace (Rom. 3:28)

        d.   We are justified by faith in Christ and have peace with God (Rom. 5:1)

  C. *Consider the Way We Will Be*

    1. These justified sinners will someday be like Jesus

        a.   While here, grace enables us to grow in the knowledge of Christ

        b.   When Christ returns, we will be like Him (1 John 3:2)

    2. This upward way is all of grace

        a.   The Holy Spirit guides us in becoming more like Jesus (Gal. 5:22–23)

        b.   Even in trials and temptations, we're guarded by His love (1 Cor. 10:13)

III. Conclusion

  A. *Can You Find Yourself in Paul's List of Lost Ones?*

  B. *Come to Faith in Jesus and Be Made Clean*

  C. *God Specializes in Getting Bad People Cleaned Up for Heaven*

Where Is God When Events Don't Make Sense?

Isaiah 64; Romans 3:24;
Galatians 4:4–5; Revelation 3:20

I. Introduction

A. *Isaiah Cried for God to Manifest Himself*
1. The prophet longs for God to meet Israel in her time of need
2. He doesn't understand why God is silent at such a time

B. *There Are Times When We Can Identify with Isaiah's Cry*
1. When innocent people die at the hands of cruel oppressors
2. When the wicked people carry out carnage and are not judged
3. When tragedy strikes our family or nation

C. *What Is God Doing While the Unthinkable Is Happening?*

II. Body

A. *He Is Extending Grace to Man (Isa. 64; Rom. 3:24)*
1. Isaiah is calling out for God to do something drastic
   a. "Oh that thou wouldest rend the heavens"
   b. "That the mountains might flow down at thy presence"
2. We may have questions about why God doesn't prevent pain
   a. We wonder why evil people seem to get away with sin
   b. We can't understand why God doesn't prevent tragedies
3. At times in the past God judged on the spot: the Flood, Babel, Sodom
4. We all deserve God's judgment, but now He waits in grace. Why?
   a. "God is not willing that any should perish" (2 Peter 3:9)

      b.   This moment is an opportunity of grace for each of us

B. *He Is Fulfilling His Plan (Gal. 4:4–5)*
1. Since before the foundations of the earth, God has had a plan
2. This plan even involved the fall of man
    a. Did you think the Fall in Eden took God by surprise?
    b. The first promise of redemption was given in Eden (Gen. 3:15)
3. Then came the long wait for the Savior
    a. The promises came through the prophets: virgin born, Emmanuel, Bethlehem
    b. Then came four hundred years of silence—then a flurry of angelic activities
    c. Christ was born (when the fullness of the time was come)
4. God is always on time
    a. He was on time at the Cross and the Resurrection
    b. He will be on time with the return of Christ
5. Are you ready for that great day?

C. *He Is Knocking with His Hand (Rev. 3:20)*
1. "Behold, I stand at the door, and knock"
2. Jesus takes the humblest place, inviting us to fellowship and eternal life
3. God's hand moves nations and circumstances to bring people to salvation
    a. Do you hear His voice?
    b. Have you recognized His work in your life?

III.   Conclusion
A. *God Will Meet You Where You Are*
B. *God Will Respond to Your Call and Give You Eternal Life*
C. *God Will Finally Make Everything Right*

Witnesses

Series on the Witnesses Begins   *Acts 1:8*

I. Introduction
- A. *Christ Held the First Missionary Conference*
  1. It was at the Lord's last meeting with His followers
  2. Christ would soon ascend to heaven
  3. Missionaries were being appointed to reach the world
- B. *A Distraction Was Dealt With*
  1. "Lord, wilt thou at this time restore again the kingdom to Israel?"
  2. We don't know the "times nor the seasons" (when Christ will return)
  3. We do know it is time to be witnesses (soul winners)
- C. *What's Witnessing All About?*

II. Body
- A. *The Lord's Witnesses Tell What They Know*
  1. "Ye shall be witnesses"
  2. This is the responsibility of any witness
     - a. A witness in court must tell what he or she knows
     - b. A witness to an accident or a crime must tell what he or she has seen
  3. If you know God loves you, tell how you know
  4. If you know Jesus has saved you, tell how you know
  5. Peter told those gathered for Pentecost what he knew about Jesus (Acts 2)
  6. Philip told the Ethiopian eunuch what he knew about Jesus (Acts 8:26–39)
  7. Paul told King Agrippa what he knew about Jesus (Acts 26)
- B. *The Lord's Witnesses Tell About Who They Know*
  1. "Ye shall be witnesses unto me"
  2. Christ is the subject of our witnessing
     - a. We are to tell lost people about the One who came to save

157

        b.   We are to tell of His miraculous birth, His life, His death on the Cross

        c.   We are to tell of His resurrection and His return

    3.   Our purpose in witnessing is to share the gospel (1 Cor. 15:3–4)

    4.   Our goal is not to impress others with our knowledge of theology

        a.   Many know the theories of theologians but don't know Jesus

        b.   Many know about the glory of heaven but are headed for hell

    5.   Our goal is to introduce people to Jesus, the only way to heaven (John 14:6)

C.   *The Lord's Witnesses Know Where to Go*

    1.   "In Jerusalem and . . . unto the uttermost part of the earth"

    2.   "The world is my parish" (John Wesley)

        a.   The same can be said of every Christian

        b.   We are to be witnesses everywhere we go as long as we live

    3.   We are to be witnesses who are always on call and on the job

        a.   We are to be witnesses in our homes and places of work

        b.   We are to be witnesses in all of our daily contacts

III. Conclusion

A.   *How Important to You Is Being a Witness?*

B.   *How Long Has It Been Since You Told Another of Jesus?*

C.   *We Will Each Give an Account of Our Witnessing (Rom. 14:12)*

Stephen: The Witnessing Deacon

I. Introduction

A. *Satan Opposed the Progress of the Early Church (Chap. 6)*
  1. Satan opposed through inward dissension (vv. 1–4)
  2. Satan opposed through outward persecution (vv. 9–15)

B. *The Church Gets Organized (6:2–8)*
  1. The leaders, unable to handle the load, appoint the first deacons
    a. The first deacons had to meet qualifications (v. 3)
    b. Stephen, a Spirit-filled man of faith, was the first chosen
  2. Proper organization brought great growth and many blessings (v. 7)

C. *What Made Stephen Such a Dynamic Witness?*

II. Body

A. *He Had Full Confidence in the Word of God (7:1–54)*
  1. When Stephen began to witness, persecution began
    a. He was called before the council to be judged
    b. False witnesses testified against him
  2. Stephen relied on the Word of God in his witness before the council
    a. His defense begins and ends with the glory of God
    b. His witness to the council is filled with Scripture
  3. It is one thing to quote verses in church and another to stake your life on them
    a. Stephen declared his faith in God's Word when to do so meant martyrdom
    b. Witnessing with Scripture guarantees our words will be effective (Isa. 55:11)

B. *He Was Fully Committed to His Savior (vv. 54–56)*
  1. The council reacted violently to Stephen's witness

          a.   The council members were filled with anger at this bold believer

          b.   They rose up against Stephen, demanding his death

    2.   We should not be surprised when the world rejects our witness

          a.   Jesus said believers would be rejected because He was rejected (John 15)

          b.   Rejection should never still our tongues from their greatest purpose

    3.   The life committed to self will shrink from the danger of witnessing

          a.   That life will be faithful as long as it is convenient

          b.   That life will be surrendered only as long as it doesn't mean sacrifice

    4.   The life committed to the Savior is bold even in the face of danger or death

    5.   The Savior met Stephen in his time of need and gave him a glimpse of glory

  C. *He Felt Compassion for the Lost (vv. 57–60)*

    1.   Heaven was real to Stephen; he looked up and saw Jesus

    2.   Jesus was standing to minister to his faithful servant

    3.   Stephen uttered a moving prayer just before his death

          a.   "Lord Jesus, receive my spirit"

          b.   "Lord, lay not this sin to their charge"

    4.   Stephen's compassionate prayer must have affected Saul, the persecutor (8:1)

III. Conclusion

  A. *Stephen's Sources of Power Were Scripture, Surrender, Souls*

  B. *What Part Do These Power Sources Play in Our Witnessing?*

  C. *Has Our Neglect of Them Kept Us from Being Dynamic Witnesses?*

Peter: The Man Who Broadened His Witness

Series on the Witnesses *Acts 10*

I. **Introduction**
    A. *Meet Cornelius: The Soldier Who Wanted Salvation*
        1. Cornelius was a centurion, heading a select troop of Italian soldiers
        2. Cornelius had many good qualities (vv. 1–2)
            a. He was a devout, God-fearing, praying man
            b. He was generous to the poor (gave charitable gifts)
        3. Cornelius was sincere and seeking . . . but lost
    B. *The Seeking Savior Saves Seeking Sinners*
        1. Cornelius is told to send men to Joppa to find Peter (vv. 3–8)
        2. There is a problem: Peter doesn't think Gentiles can be saved
    C. *Peter's Witness—and Ours—Needed Broadening*

II. **Body**
    A. *God Gets Peter Ready to Broaden His Witness (vv. 9–18)*
        1. Peter was already a successful witness
            a. On Pentecost, he preached and had three thousand converts (chap. 2)
            b. At the temple, he had prayed and brought healing to a lame man (chap. 3)
            c. After his second sermon, five thousand were saved (3:12–4:4)
        2. Now Peter is given a vision to broaden his witnessing to include Gentiles
            a. He must see that the gospel is for everyone (John 3:16)
            b. He must remove the limits on his witnessing (Rom. 10:9–13)
        3. What limits your witnessing horizons? Who are you excluding from grace?
    B. *God Gives Peter Reasons to Broaden His Witness (vv. 19–33)*

161

    1. The Holy Spirit gave Peter guidance concerning those sent from Cornelius
        a. These were prospects for broadening his witness: "Behold three men seek thee"
        b. Successful witnessing begins in faith: "Go with them, doubting nothing"
    2. Peter learned about the work of God in the life of Cornelius
        a. He found out about the character of Cornelius
        b. He was told of God's warning to Cornelius that he needed more than works
    3. Cornelius had a crowd waiting, increasing Peter's opportunities (v. 24)
    4. Cornelius was receptive to Peter and his message (v. 25)
    5. Peter explains God's work in his heart that prepared him to witness (vv. 26–29)
    6. Cornelius explains God's work in his life that prepared him to hear the gospel (vv. 30–33)
    7. When God moves us to witness, He prepares our hearers to receive the message

  C. *God Grants Peter Results from His Broadened Witnessing (vv. 34–48)*
    1. Peter presents the gospel to Cornelius (vv. 34–43)
        a. He explains the basics of God's salvation
        b. He tells of the death and resurrection of Christ
    2. Peter quotes the prophets and their promise of salvation by faith
    3. Cornelius and his friends are converted (vv. 44–48)
    4. Joy and fellowship follow effective witnessing (v. 48)

III. Conclusion
  A. *A Whole New World of Witnessing Opened to Peter*
  B. *God Wants to Broaden the Scope of Your Witnessing*
  C. *There Is Joy for Every Believer in Increased Outreach (Ps. 126:6)*

Paul: The Witness to All

Series on the Witnesses *Acts 9:1–20*

I. Introduction
- A. *Paul Hated Witnessing Christians*
    1. He had approved the stoning of Stephen (Acts 7:58–8:1)
    2. He made every effort to destroy the infant church (vv. 1–2)
- B. *Meeting Jesus on the Road to Damascus Changed Paul for Life*
    1. "Lord, what wilt thou have me to do?" (v. 6)
    2. "Arise, and go," started Paul going and he kept witnessing for life (v. 6)
- C. *Ananias Received a Revelation Concerning Paul (vv. 10–16)*

II. Body
- A. *Paul Would Be a Chosen Witness (v. 15)*
    1. Paul had been stricken blind during his encounter with Christ
    2. Ananias was to pray for him and restore his sight
        a. Ananias was reluctant (vv. 13–14)
        b. The Lord reassured Ananias
    3. This witness would suffer many things because of his faith
        a. He would be beaten and imprisoned (2 Cor. 11:23–24)
        b. Like Stephen, he would be stoned for his witnessing (11:25)
        c. He would live in peril of his life, yet keep witnessing (11:26–27)
    4. Paul's witnessing would be clearly defined
        a. He would continually major on the Cross (1 Cor. 2:2)
        b. He would witness about the Resurrection and the power of Christ to save (1 Cor. 15)
- B. *Paul Would Witness to Gentiles and Government Leaders (v. 15)*

163

1. He would "bear the name of Christ" to the Gentiles
    a. Paul would be the greatest missionary of all time
    b. Neither persecution, privation, nor pain could stop him
2. Paul's witnessing journeys would bring many to Jesus
3. A prophecy was given to Ananias about Paul witnessing before rulers
    a. Paul witnessed to Felix and Festus (Acts 24–25)
    b. Paul witnessed to King Agrippa (Acts 25–26)
4. Give Paul the floor anytime and he will witness about his conversion
    a. He witnessed with passion, power, and tears (Acts 20:20, 31)
    b. How long has it been since you seized an opportunity to witness?

C. *Paul Would Witness to the Jews (v. 15)*
1. Ananias was told that Paul would witness "to the children of Israel"
2. Paul witnessed often in synagogues (v. 20; 17:2–3)
    a. His method: he reasoned with them out of the Scriptures (v. 2)
    b. His message: Christ suffered, died, and rose again (v. 3)
    c. His invitation: Christ is the only Savior for Jews and Gentiles (Rom. 1:16)
3. Paul had a heartfelt burden for the salvation of his people (Rom. 9:1–3; 10:1–4)

III. Conclusion

A. *Consider the "Alls" of Paul's Call*
1. He saw all people as sinners and Christ their only hope (Rom. 3:10–26)
2. He became all things to all men that by all means he might save some (1 Cor. 9:22)

B. *Let's Follow Paul by Witnessing to All (1 Cor. 11:1)*

Barnabas: Who Witnessed to the Body of Christ

Series on the Witnesses   *Acts 4:36–37; 9:26–27; 11:22–25*

I. **Introduction**
   A. *Witnessing Is Usually Connected with Evangelism*
      1. Peter witnessed on the day of Pentecost (Acts 2)
      2. Paul witnessed to the Philippian jailer (Acts 16)
   B. *Witnessing Can Also Be to the Body of Christ*
      1. This kind of witnessing builds faith among believers
      2. This kind of witnessing strengthens churches
   C. *Barnabas Witnessed to the Body of Christ*

II. **Body**
   A. *Barnabas Witnessed by Giving (Acts 4:36–37)*
      1. There were difficult circumstances in the church at Jerusalem
         a. Most had come for Passover and had been converted on Pentecost
         b. Many of these converts stayed, needing more supplies to survive
         c. They demonstrated their love by pooling their resources
      2. Some of these new believers were becoming discouraged
         a. Joses encouraged so many they called him Barnabas (encourager)
         b. "I would like to have a name like that. I would like to be the means of consolation to God's people" (H. A. Ironside)
      4. Barnabas sold his land and gave the money to the church to meet the needs of others
      5. Barnabas was "as one designed to be a preacher of the gospel, he disentangled himself from the affairs of this life" (Matthew Henry)
   B. *Barnabas Witnessed by Greeting (Acts 9:26–27)*
      1. The conversion of Saul was a key to the growth of the early church

       a. Saul was transformed from a murderer to a missionary

       b. He was changed from a persecutor to a preacher of the gospel

  2. When Saul came to Jerusalem to meet the disciples, they were afraid of him

       a. "Believers are apt to be too suspicious of those of whom they have prejudices. . . . It is necessary to be cautious but we must exercise charity" (Matthew Henry)

       b. These fearful disciples nearly rejected the greatest missionary of all time

  3. Barnabas took the lead in greeting Saul and urging others to do so

       a. "The testimony of Barnabas authenticated the testimony of Saul" (H. A. Ironside)

       b. Barnabas was a peacemaker between Saul and the other disciples

  4. We need believers like Barnabas who will welcome others into the family of God

C. *Barnabas Witnessed by Going (Acts 11:22–26; 13:1–2)*

  1. When the revival at Antioch took place, Barnabas was sent to report the results

       a. Leaders of the church knew Barnabas would be willing to go

       b. The church suffers from lack of people willing to go

  2. Barnabas saw he needed help so went to Tarsus to get Saul (v. 25)

  3. The revival was so real Barnabas and Saul stayed and taught for a year

  4. The disciples were first called "Christians" during the work of Barnabas and Saul

III. Conclusion

A. *Are You Witnessing by Giving, Greeting, and Going?*

B. *What Would Happen in Our Church If We Witnessed Like Barnabas?*

C. *Let's Make Our Church a Fellowship of Encouragers*

Dorcas: Who Witnessed with Deeds

Series on the Witnesses   *Acts 9:36–42*

I. Introduction

A. *The Early Church Was Put on the Move*
   1. Thousands were saved at Jerusalem and beyond
   2. Saul was saved on the road to Damascus
   3. The gospel spread through Judea, Galilee, and Samaria

B. *Peter Performed Miracles at Lydda and Joppa (vv. 32–43)*
   1. The palsied man was healed at Lydda
   2. Peter raised Dorcas from the dead in Joppa

C. *Who Is Dorcas and What Did She Do?*

II. Body

A. *Dorcas Was a Disciple (v. 36)*
   1. Dorcas is the Greek form of her Aramaic name, Tabitha
   2. The Holy Spirit identifies her as a disciple
      a. She had seen herself as a sinner and trusted Christ as her Savior
      b. She was dedicated to Christ and followed Him in daily life
   3. The fruit of the Spirit was evident in the life of Dorcas
      a. Her testimony was no empty profession; others saw Christ in her
      b. Her faith was living and bearing fruit that blessed other believers
   4. Good works should flow from our faith (Eph. 2:8–10)
      a. Jesus said our good works would glorify our Father in heaven (Matt. 5:16)
      b. How has your conduct changed since your conversion to Christ? (2 Cor. 5:17)

B. *Dorcas Was Diligent (v. 36)*
   1. She was "full of good works and almsdeeds"
      a. The mercy of Christ was demonstrated through her

167

b.   She saw people as God sees them—in need of His love

2.   The hands of Dorcas became the hands of her Lord
a.   She was always reaching out to the needy
b.   Widows found those hands providing hands

3.   When Dorcas died, the needy felt her loss
a.   She had been there when they were destitute
b.   She had ministered to them in love

4.   The hands of Dorcas were witnessing hands
a.   She had a dedicated needle
b.   Her hands spoke of the love of Jesus

C.   *Dorcas Was Delivered (vv. 38–42)*
1.   When Dorcas died, the disciples sent for Peter
2.   Peter came, knowing that faithful Dorcas had died
a.   The circumstances must have reminded him of Jesus going to raise Lazarus (John 11)
b.   The weeping ones brought back the memory of Lazarus's family and friends
3.   Peter called Dorcas back to life: "Tabitha, arise," and she arose!

III.   Conclusion
A.   *As a Disciple, Dorcas Witnessed of the Saving Power of Christ*
B.   *In Her Deeds, Dorcas Witnessed of the Compassion of Christ*
C.   *Do Our Deeds Witness of the Love and Compassion of Jesus for All?*

Lydia: Who Witnessed Through Hospitality

Series on the Witnesses   *Acts 16:13–15, 40*

I. Introduction

  A. *Lydia Is the Woman Who Met Paul and Silas at a Prayer Meeting (v. 13)*

   1. Good things happen when you meet with others to pray

   2. Lydia went to the prayer meeting and had her best day

  B. *Paul and Silas Preached at a Small Meeting by the River*

   1. They didn't require a big crowd to minister God's Word

   2. They opened the Scriptures and found receptive hearers

  C. *Meet Lydia: A Woman Ready to Do Business with God*

II. Body

  A. *Lydia Opened Her Ears (v. 14)*

   1. Lydia was a businesswoman—a seller of purple

    a. She was a Gentile from Thyatira, now living in Philippi

    b. She had been seeking the Lord, so she came to a Jewish prayer meeting

   2. Lydia worshiped God but didn't really know Him

    a. Many in churches today are like Lydia

    b. Are you one of them?

   3. Lydia was a good listener

    a. Nothing could distract her from Paul's message

    b. Luke says Lydia "heard us"

   4. Many are exposed to good preaching but don't pay attention

   5. How many sermons have you sat through without really hearing them?

  B. *The Lord Opened Lydia's Heart (v. 14)*

   1. Those who seek the Lord find Him (Jer. 29:13)

   2. Lydia listened and God opened her heart

    a. "Whose heart the Lord opened"

   b. When Lydia's heart was open, she responded
to the gospel
3. A Gentile woman at a Jewish prayer meeting came
to Jesus
   a. God meets us where we are and opens our
hearts to His Word
   b. What good news this must have been to Lydia!
4. A searching woman found the Savior and
surrendered all
   a. Lydia was the first convert in Europe
   b. She made her conversion public through
baptism, as did her family
C. *Lydia Opened Her Home (vv. 15, 40)*
1. The new Lydia invited Paul, Silas, and Luke to her
home
   a. "If ye have judged me to be faithful to the
Lord"
   b. Lydia pleaded her newfound faith as a reason
for fellowship
2. Hospitality is a powerful means of witness
   a. This saleswoman "constrained" these
preachers to come to her home
   b. She wanted her family and neighbors to know
what had happened
3. After the prison revival, the preachers and their
converts were invited again (v. 40)

III. **Conclusion**
   A. *Hospitality Is a Wonderful Way to Show Christian
Love*
   B. *How Many of the Family of God Have You Invited to
Your Home?*
   C. *Let's Make Our Homes Centers for Fellowship and
Evangelism*

John: The Witness of Love

Series on the Witnesses Ends   *1 John 3:1, 14–18; 4:9–10*

I. Introduction
   A. *John's Writings Are the Favorite of Many*
      1. Millions of copies of the gospel of John have been printed and distributed
      2. The work of John is used for evangelism and Christian growth
      3. New converts are often advised to read the gospel of John first
   B. *The Scope of John's Witnessing Was Wide*
      1. In his gospel, he chronicled the life of Jesus
      2. In his epistles, he taught how to live with assurance of salvation
      3. In Revelation, he revealed God's prophetic plan
   C. *Love Flows Through John's Witnessing*

II. Body
   A. *John Witnessed About God's Love for Us (3:1)*
      1. "Behold, what manner of love the Father hath bestowed upon us"
      2. John was first introduced to Christ (Matt. 4:21)
         a. Jesus called to James and John while they were fishing
         b. There was something about that call of love that John couldn't resist
      3. John learned about love
         a. He wanted the Lord to call down fire on a Samaritan city (Luke 9:51–56)
         b. He observed the Lord's love for the woman at the well (John 4:1–30)
         c. He witnessed the Lord's love for the woman taken in adultery (John 8:1–12)
      4. Watching Jesus, John saw God's love in action; so can we
   B. *John Witnessed About Our Love for Others (3:14–18)*
      1. As proof we have passed from death to life, we love the brethren
         a. Here is a mark of salvation that is unmistakable

        b. We cannot love God and hate brothers and sisters in Christ

    2. Here are some strong words: "He that loveth not his brother abideth in death . . . is a murderer"

        a. We can know all the facts of the gospel and be spiritually dead

        b. Our spiritual temperature is revealed on the thermometer of love

    3. Love for other Christians is measured by our kindness to them

        a. We are to lay down our lives for those in the family of God

        b. When they are in need, we are to help them from our resources

    4. Selfishness is the opposite of love (1 Cor. 13)

C. *John Witnessed About the Greatest Example of Love (4:9–10)*

    1. The Cross is the greatest example of God's love

        a. John had stood at the Cross and been commissioned there (John 19:25–27)

        b. He learned that God loved him and had work for him to do

    2. "God sent his only begotten Son into the world"

        a. Writing these words must have reminded him of John 3:16

        b. The message of the Cross is the message of salvation

    3. God's love is demonstrated in the death of Christ for us (v. 10)

III. Conclusion

A. *How Long Has It Been Since You Told Someone of God's Love?*

B. *What Have You Done to Show Your Love for Other Christians?*

C. *Does the Love of God Motivate and Empower Your Witnessing?*

Good News for a Desperate Deputy

Acts 13:6–12

I. **Introduction**
   A. *Paul Embarks on the First Missionary Journey*
      1. Missionary work would be the fulfillment of God's purpose in Saul's life
      2. Saul and Barnabas were called by the Lord and sent by the church at Antioch
         a. The church at Antioch birthed the first great missionary movement
         b. Mark accompanied Saul and Barnabas on this important journey
   B. *He Sailed to Cyprus to Minister Where Barnabas Had Been Born*
      1. He preached in the synagogues at Salamis, ministering to the Jews first (Rom. 1:16)
      2. He met two men to remember at Paphos
         a. Bar-jesus was a Jewish sorcerer who would oppose and distract them
         b. Sergius Paulus was a deputy who would welcome them and bring them delight

II. **Body**
   A. *The Deputy Had a Desire (v. 7)*
      1. He desired to hear the Word of God
      2. The deputy (proconsul) was an important man
         a. He was similar to a governor but with a limited term
         b. He is called prudent (intelligent, sensible)
      3. This important man knew he needed God
         a. He was aware of the limitations of human power
         b. He desperately wanted to hear a word from the Lord
      4. Do you desire to hear what God has to say to you?
   B. *The Deputy Was Distracted (vv. 6–11)*
      1. Enter Elymas (Bar-jesus), who tried to distract the deputy
      2. Who was this distracter?

173

       a. He was a Jew, a false prophet, and a sorcerer (v. 6)

       b. He called himself Bar-jesus (son of Jesus)

       c. He tried to distract the deputy from coming to faith in Christ

    3. Distraction often comes from those professing special gifts from God

    4. Saul boldly rebuked this enemy of the truth (vv. 9–10)

       a. He called him a deceiver and corrupter of the truth

       b. He called him a child of the Devil and an enemy of righteousness

       c. Servants of God must boldly denounce sin and false teachings

    5. Elymus was stricken blind for his sinful opposition to the truth

  C. *The Deputy Made a Decision (v. 12)*

    1. When he saw what happened to Elymus, he believed

       a. He saw that false teaching leads to blindness

       b. He turned from false doctrine to faith in Christ

    2. The deputy was astonished at what Saul said about Jesus

       a. The gospel was truly good news to him

       b. The death and resurrection of Christ captured his heart

III. Conclusion

  A. *After the Deputy's Conversion, Saul's Name Was Changed to Paul*

  B. *"Paul Took the Name of His Illustrious Convert" (H. A. Ironside)*

  C. *When We Lead Others to Christ, We Are Changed Too*

Paul's Long Sermon in the Synagogue

Acts 13:14–46

I. Introduction
  A. *Consider the Two Antiochs*
    1. Paul and Barnabas had been sent from the church at Antioch east of the Mediterranean
    2. Now they minister at Antioch north of the Mediterranean in Pisidia near Galatia
    3. Great works of God began and were established in both Antiochs
  B. *The Stranger in the Synagogue Begins His Powerful Sermon*
    1. Paul shows the Jews all their history is His-story
    2. He told His-story from Moses in Egypt to Joshua in Canaan (vv. 16–19)
    3. He told His-story from the times of the judges to John the Baptist (vv. 20–25)
      a. Christ the Son of David is the promised Savior (vv. 22–23)
      b. John the Baptist's Lord and Lamb fulfill Isaiah's prophecies (vv. 24–28)
  C. *Logical Conclusions Were Drawn from All This Information*

II. Body
  A. *Christ Is the Figure of Forgiveness (v. 38)*
    1. The gospel is the good news of forgiveness for all people
    2. "Men and brethren"
      a. It is forgiveness for Paul's brethren, the Jews
      b. It is forgiveness for Gentiles as well (v. 42)
    3. We all need forgiveness because we are all sinners (Rom. 3:10–23)
      a. Righteous acts cannot atone for sins (Isa. 64:6)
      b. Only Christ can cleanse and make us clean (1 John 1:9)
  B. *There Are Priceless Benefits of Believing (v. 39)*
    1. "By him [Christ] all that believe are justified"
    2. Justification goes beyond forgiveness

175

           a.   Forgiveness clears our sinful record

           b.   Justification declares us righteous (as if we'd never sinned)

      3.   There are priceless results of being justified

           a.   We have peace with God (Rom. 5:1)

           b.   We are saved from wrath (Rom. 5:9)

           c.   We are not condemned (Rom. 8:1, 33)

      4.   These benefits are not available through law keeping (Rom. 3:20; Gal. 2:16)

           a.   They are available by faith because of Christ's death (Gal. 3:6–11)

           b.   They are available to all sinners through faith (1 Cor. 6:9–11)

    C.   *There Is Danger of Doubting (vv. 40–41)*

      1.   Here is a solemn word of warning for those who reject the message

      2.   "Beware therefore"

           a.   The offer of salvation by grace is a great privilege

           b.   To reject this offer brings greater condemnation

      3.   To receive Christ is to live . . . to reject Him is to perish (John 3:36)

III.   Conclusion

    A.   *Paul's Hearers Responded to the Good News*

      1.   Some believed and were eager to hear more (vv. 42–44)

      2.   Some doubted and spoke evil of Paul and Barnabas (v. 45)

    B.   *What Is Your Response to the Gospel Today?*

Saints Alive!

Ephesians 1:1; 5:3; Revelation 13:7; Jude 14

I. Introduction
A. *Who Are the Saints?*
   1. The dictionary defines a saint
      a. A saint is a holy or godly person
      b. A saint is a very patient, unselfish person
      c. In the New Testament, a saint is any Christian believer
   2. The Bible agrees with the third definition
B. *Saints Are Alive and Known Today*
   1. Saints are not just those declared to be so after death
   2. How do we know this is true?

II. Body
A. *Paul Wrote to the Saints (Eph. 1:1)*
   1. We only write letters to the living
   2. Paul wrote to church members who were alive at that time
   3. These letters had to do with personal relationships
      a. Pastors and others were instructed to "perfect" the saints (Eph. 4:12)
      b. Money was to be distributed to help the poor saints (Rom. 12:13)
   4. Paul, before his conversion, had imprisoned saints (Acts 26:10)
      a. Later he was also imprisoned (a saint in a prison cell)
      b. In places of persecution, many saints are still imprisoned
   5. Clearly, every believer is a saint
B. *The Bible Outlines the Responsibilities of the Saints (Eph. 5:3)*
   1. Here is a great text for Christian living (Eph. 5:1–10)
   2. Here is the key to understanding this kind of holy living
      a. "As becometh saints"

177

        b.   We are to live holy because we are saints
    3.   Saints ought to live saintly
        a.   We are to be saints early in the morning and late at night
        b.   We are to be saints when walking, talking, driving, etc.
    4.   Saints are to represent their Savior at all times

C. *The Wrath of the Antichrist Will Be Against the Saints (Rev. 13:7)*
    1.   There are difficult days ahead for Tribulation saints
    2.   Many are to be martyred during that terrible time
    3.   Trials of most saints today are small in comparison (Rev. 16:6)
    4.   Saints are to overcome then and now by the blood of the Lamb (Rev. 12:11)

D. *The Saints Will Return with Christ to Reign (Jude 14)*
    1.   Walking with God enabled Enoch to see the future coming kingdom
    2.   The saints will come riding in (Rev. 19:11–16)
    3.   The saints will rule and reign with their Savior King (Rev. 20:6)

III. Conclusion

A. *In Every Age, God Has a Remnant That Represents Him*

B. *The Saints Represent Their Savior in the Present Evil World*
    1.   What kind of a representative of Jesus are you?
    2.   What needs to change to make your life conform to your position as a saint?

The Regions Beyond

2 Corinthians 10:16

I. **Introduction**
   A. *Paul Shares His Heart's Desire*
      1. He gives these Corinthian saints a look inside his heart
      2. He lets them know what motivates him to keep pressing on
   B. *The Greatest Missionary Wants to Extend His Borders*
      1. He wants to break new ground for Jesus
      2. He longs to preach the gospel in the regions beyond
   C. *Consider These Questions About Paul's Great Desire*

II. **Body**
   A. *Why Did Paul Want to Go to the Regions Beyond?*
      1. He was convinced of the lost condition of all people (Rom. 3:10–23)
         a. Paul placed no limits on his responsibility for outreach
         b. Paul felt responsible to reach lost souls everywhere (Rom. 1:14–16)
         c. Moody witnessed to at least one lost person daily
      2. Consider Paul's caring questions (Rom. 10:13–15)
         a. How shall they call on Him in whom they have not believed?
         b. How shall they believe in Him of whom they have not heard?
         c. How shall they hear without a preacher?
         d. How shall they preach unless they be sent?
      3. Paul's driving desire was to reach the unreached
      4. What is the driving desire in your life?
   B. *What Did Paul Want to Tell Those in the Regions Beyond?*
      1. He longed to tell them of God's love for sinners (Rom. 5:8)
         a. What a revolutionary message!
         b. God's love moves one from religion to a relationship with God

179

           c.   God's love extends grace to guilty people deserving of hell

     2.   Paul longed to give lost people the gospel (1 Cor. 15:3–4)

           a.   Christ died for our sins *according to the Scriptures*

           b.   Christ was buried *according to the Scriptures*

           c.   Christ rose again *according to the Scriptures*

           d.   This message is authenticated by the Word of God

     3.   Like Paul, we ought to have a motivating passion to tell this good news to sinners

  C. *Where Do the Regions Beyond Begin?*

     1.   The regions beyond begin just beyond your present area of witness

           a.   They begin just beyond your front door

           b.   They begin just beyond the church door

           c.   They begin just beyond your last testimony to any sinner

     2.   Paul wanted to go beyond any place he had ever gone before

           a.   How far into your mission field have you ventured?

           b.   How far are you willing to go?

III. Conclusion

  A. *Are You Willing to Break Out of Your Comfort Zone?*

  B. *Are You Willing to Have God Increase Your Outreach?*

  C. *Are You Willing to Go to the Regions Beyond?*

Thanksgiving and Peace

Thanksgiving   *Philippians 4:6–7*

I. Introduction
  A. *Three Kinds of Peace Are Mentioned in the Bible*
    1. Peace with God comes at salvation (Rom. 5:1)
    2. The peace of God comes with surrender (Phil. 4:7)
    3. Peace on earth will come at Christ's second coming (Isa. 2:1–4)
  B. *Our Focus Today Is on the Peace of God*
    1. It is peace in times of trouble
    2. Paul says we are to stop worrying
       a. Easier said than done
       b. The key is having a thankful heart
  C. *Why Is Thanksgiving the Key to Peace?*

II. Body
  A. *Thanksgiving Calls for Looking Up*
    1. Storms in life may make thanksgiving difficult
    2. We all go through times of trouble (John 16:33)
    3. The Pilgrims endured many hardships
       a. Sickness, loneliness—nearly half died the first winter
       c. A drought in summer caused them to look up
       d. A gentle rain came in answer to prayer
    4. A good harvest resulted in the first Thanksgiving
    5. Looking up to our Helper makes us thankful people
  B. *Thanksgiving Calls for Looking Around*
    1. We all have many blessings and ought to give thanks for them
    2. Consider Psalm 103, the psalm of thanksgiving
       a. "Forget not all his benefits"
       b. Those benefits include sins forgiven, daily health, food, family, friends
    3. We ought to start each day, thankful for His many benefits
       a. The benefits of God's love and grace
       b. The benefit of salvation by faith
       c. The benefit of having a Bible

181

    4. We have the privilege of prayer
        a. We do not have to be anxious because prayer makes God's blessings available
        b. Thanksgiving adds expectation to prayer and allows faith to expect answers

  C. *Thanksgiving Calls for Looking Ahead*
    1. Doubt cringes and cowers, afraid of what tomorrow may bring
    2. Faith welcomes the future with optimism, expecting the best
    3. Paul reveals what a thankful heart contains
        a. It contains things that are true, honest, just, pure, lovely, good, virtuous
        b. Thanksgiving allows us to believe the best is yet to come
    4. Is your mind a place for thankful thoughts to dwell?

III. Conclusion

  A. *How Do You React to Looking Up, Around, and Ahead?*
  B. *Do These Realities Frighten You?*
  C. *Ask God for a Heart That Appreciates His Blessings Every Day*

Thanksgiving: The Secret of Contentment

Thanksgiving   *1 Timothy 6:6*

I. **Introduction**
   A. *The Whole World Seeks Contentment*
      1. Some hope to gain contentment through wealth or success
      2. Some hope to gain contentment through personal achievements
      3. Many wealthy, successful, and honored people are not content
   B. *A Thankful Heart Is the Key to Contentment*
      1. Thankful people have discovered how to be content
      2. See my book *Staying Positive in a Negative World* (Grand Rapids: Kregel, 1997)
   C. *Why Thankful People Are Content*

II. **Body**
   A. *Thankful People Rejoice in What They Have*
      1. "Be content with such things as you have" (Heb. 13:5)
         a. This is the key to conquering covetousness
         b. Contentment frees us from lusting for possessions
      2. Paul was content because he was continually thankful (1 Thess. 5:18)
         a. A thankful heart made him contented all the time (Phil. 4:11–12)
         b. His contentment was not based on what he had (v. 12)
         c. Christ made him content in all conditions (v. 13)
      3. Thankful people recognize the transience of all things
         a. We were born broke and will die the same way
         b. Having food and clothing, we can be content (1 Tim. 6:7–8)

  B. *Thankful People Refuse to Be Ruled by What They Don't Have*

     1. The desire to be rich rules many people

        a. This leads to being caught in the Devil's trap

        b. Longing to be rich is "A temptation and a snare" (1 Tim. 6:9)

     2. The love of money is the root of all evil (6:10)

        a. The love of money cost the rich young ruler his soul (Luke 18:23)

        b. Breaking free from the love of money brought salvation to Zacchaeus (Luke 19:1–10)

     3. Chasing dreams of money and possessions is costly

        a. Many spend years in prison for trying to cash in unlawfully

        b. Many lose their families and reputations in the money chase

     4. Are you ruled by things you crave but do not have?

  C. *Thankful People Recognize God Gives Us All We Have*

     1. "Godliness with contentment is great gain" (1 Tim. 6:6)

        a. Cash without Christ caters only to carnality

        b. Possessions without the Prince of Peace never satisfy

     2. Contentment comes from knowing and serving Christ

        a. Responding to His love in faith brings new life

        b. Remembering we are but sinners saved by grace makes us thankful

     3. Everything we have is from our loving Savior's hand (James 1:17)

III. Conclusion

  A. *Are You a Contented Christian?*

  B. *Do Others Recognize the Reason for Your Peace?*

  C. *Your Contentment Can Draw Others to Your Lord*

Death Doesn't Get the Last Word

Series on Heaven Begins   *1 Corinthians 15:55–57*

I. Introduction
A. *Death Is the Subject We'd Like to Avoid*
1. No one likes to think about death
2. Why dwell on something so dreadful?

B. *Death Is an Enemy (1 Cor. 15:26)*
1. Death is unnatural; we were created to live
2. Death came because of sin (Rom. 5:12; 6:23)
3. Jesus wept at a grave (John 11:35)
a. Weeping demonstrates the pain of death to loved ones
b. Graves remind us that death stalks us all (Heb. 9:27)

C. *But Death Doesn't Get the Last Word*

II. Body
A. *Salvation Says Death Doesn't Get the Last Word*
1. Jesus came to restore what was lost because of sin
a. He came to seek and save the lost (Luke 19:10)
b. He came to bring life to dying sinners (John 11:25)
2. Jesus conquered two kinds of death
a. He conquered spiritual death (Eph. 2:5–9)
b. He conquered physical death (1 Cor. 15:55–57)
3. Faith in Christ brings everlasting life (John 3:16)
4. Everlasting life is a present possession of believers (John 3:36; 1 John 5:12)

B. *Heaven Says Death Doesn't Get the Last Word*
1. Salvation changes the destination of the soul, ending death's power
2. The saved go to heaven when they die
a. To die is gain (Phil. 1:21)
b. To depart and be with Christ is far better (Phil. 1:23)
3. Christians are with the Lord at death (2 Cor. 5:8)
4. Heaven is better than earth (John 14:1–3)

        a.   Jesus has prepared places for us in heaven
        b.   Loved ones who died in Christ await us in heaven
        c.   We will see Jesus and spend eternity with Him

C. *Resurrection Says Death Doesn't Get the Last Word*
   1.   There are great guarantees in Christ's resurrection
        a.   We are guaranteed our Savior (Rom. 1:4)
        b.   We are guaranteed our salvation (1 Cor. 15:14–20)
        c.   We are guaranteed our similar resurrection (v. 20)
   2.   Christ will resurrect our bodies (1 Thess. 4:13–18)
        a.   Our resurrection bodies will never feel pain
        b.   We will be like Jesus (1 John 3:1–2)
   3.   Suffering now cannot compare with the glory later (Rom. 8:18)

III. Conclusion

A. *Remember Paul's Two Taunting Questions of Death (v. 55)*
B. *Christ's Conquest of Death Assures Us of Victory*
C. *The Conqueror Deserves Our Service and Devotion (v. 58)*

Present with the Lord

2 Corinthians 5:8

I. Introduction

    A. *We Live in Temporary Temples*
1. Our time on earth is limited
2. We have seventy to eighty years, more or less (Ps. 90:10)
3. Medical science hasn't been able to abolish death

    B. *Paul Had Confidence Concerning His Coming Death*
1. He would be absent from his weak body
2. He would be present with his strong Lord

    C. *What Will It Mean to Be Present with the Lord?*

II. Body

    A. *We'll Be Released from the Restrictions of the Body*
1. Our bodies are wonders of Creation (Gen. 2:7)
   a. Made from the dust of the ground
   b. Given life by the breath of God
2. We are "fearfully and wonderfully made" (Ps. 139:14)
   a. We are walking miracles from the Creator's hand
   b. Medical researchers marvel at our complexity
3. Still, life in the body has its limits
   a. Poor health and handicaps may hold us back
   b. Age accentuates our limitations
4. When present with the Lord, these restrictions will end

    B. *We'll Be Received into the Realms of Glory*
1. We will undergo a great change: absent from the body, present with the Lord
   a. We will undergo a negative followed by a powerful positive
   b. Death here below means life up above
2. Being present with the Lord means arriving in heaven
   a. There are no doubts about where Jesus is—heaven
   b. After His resurrection, He ascended into heaven

  c. We'll be with Him following our last breath
 3. Descriptions of heaven fall short
  a. We've never seen any place like heaven
  b. We've never imagined any place like heaven
 4. Heaven will then be our home
C. *We'll Rejoice with the Redeemed of the Ages*
 1. Think of spending eternity with heroes of the faith
  a. We'll meet those in God's great hall of fame (Heb. 11)
  b. These giants for God will be our eternal companions
 2. We'll never tire of rejoicing in redemption (Rev. 5:9)
 3. "Worthy is the Lamb" will be our hymn to Him

III. Conclusion
A. *What Does All This Have to Do with Life Today?*
 1. Every dark day should be brightened by the prospect of heaven
 2. Every burden should be lightened by the promise of what's ahead
B. *Are You Sure of Heaven? Settle That Question Today*

Beyond Our Wildest Dreams

Series on Heaven   *1 Corinthians 2:9–10*

I. Introduction

    A. *This Text Is About the Future of Every Christian*

        1. This text inspires hope

        2. This text increases expectation

        3. This text seems too good to be true

    B. *This Text Is About Heaven*

        1. This text stretches the imagination

        2. This text describes the fantastic future of the
faithful

II. Body

    A. *Consider Our Dream Future*

        1. Most of us have dreams

            a. We dream about meeting a special person

            b. We dream abut financial success

            c. We dream about a beautiful family and home

        2. Some dreams come true and some fall short of
expectations

            a. Some succeed and others fail

            b. Some gain true riches and others lose what
counts

        3. Faith in Christ introduces us to new dreams

            a. These goals couldn't be reached without Him

            b. We have fellowship unknown apart from the
family of God

            c. We have an eternal hope the world doesn't
understand

    B. *Our Future Goes Beyond Our Wildest Dreams*

        1. It is futile, trying to describe heaven

        2. "Eye hath not seen"

            a. We've never seen anything like heaven

            b. Take your dream trip around the world, and it
will fall short of heaven

            c. Retrieve all your best memories and they
won't measure up

        3. "Nor ear heard"

            a. We've never heard of a place as wonderful as
heaven

        b.   The most eloquent speakers can't describe heaven

        c.   The greatest artists cannot paint heaven, nor composers write its music

    4.   "Neither have entered into the heart of man"

        a.   All dreams fall short of what awaits in heaven

        b.   Imagination fails to grasp the glories of our home above

C. *Our Dream Home Has Been Prepared by God Himself*

    1.   "The things which God hath prepared for them that love him."

    2.   Heaven has been prepared for those who trust in Jesus (John 14:1–3)

    3.   How great our Father's love!

        a.   His love meets us where we are (Rom. 5:8)

        b.   His love guarantees eternal life (1 John 5:11–13)

III.   Conclusion

A. *The Holy Spirit Grants a Glimpse of Glory (v. 10)*

B. *He Opens the Bible, Letting Us in on the Dream*

C. *Open Your Heart and Let the Savior In (Rev. 3:20)*

Heaven's Song

Series on Heaven *Revelation 5:9–10*

I. Introduction
A. *What Awaits Us in Heaven?*
1. This is a question with many answers
   a. Heaven is a place of beauty, of praise, of comfort, of rest, of rejoicing
   b. Heaven is where we'll meet Jesus, angels, loved ones, saints of ages past
2. Heaven is also a place of singing, so get ready to join the choir
3. "'Twill be no sad day when Christ I meet, each day I live I wait and long to place my feet on heaven's street, and hear the angel choir's song" (Roger Campbell)

B. *What Kind of Songs Will We Sing in Heaven?*
1. We have no clues as to the tempo and tunes of heaven
2. The message is all that's clear: it's the story that matters in glory

II. Body
A. *Heaven's Song Will Be About the Redeemer (v. 9)*
1. The seven sealed book is in the hand of God (v. 1)
   a. A search is made for one who was worthy to open the book (vv. 2–4)
   b. No man on earth or in heaven was found worthy
2. The One who is worthy is revealed (vv. 5–8)
   a. He is the Lion of the tribe of Judah: Jesus
   b. He is the Root of David: Jesus
   c. He is the Lamb that had been slain: Jesus
3. Our song in heaven will be about the worthy One: Jesus

B. *Heaven's Song Will Be About Redemption (v. 9)*
1. "Thou wast slain, and hast redeemed us to God"
2. We will never tire of singing about the old story
   a. The story is of lost sinners saved by the blood of Christ that was shed on the Cross

           b.   The story is of redeemed sinners made clean by the power of the gospel

      3.   "We shall have the society of all the pure and holy, made pure by the blood of Jesus. But notice carefully what they sing up there. They ascribe their redemption entirely to the Lamb of God and His work" (H. A. Ironside, *Lectures on Revelation* [Neptune, N.J.: Loizeaux, 1990], 96)

      4.   John the Baptist wrote the first verse of heaven's song: "Behold the Lamb of God which taketh away the sins of the world" (John 1:29)

    C.   *Heaven's Song Will Be About Reigning with the Redeemer (v. 10)*

      1.   "We shall reign on the earth"

      2.   Who are these who will reign with Christ?

           a.   They are but sinners saved by grace through faith (Eph. 2:8–9)

           b.   They have been transformed by the power of Christ (2 Cor. 5:17)

      3.   God's love has made lost ones into kings and priests of God

           a.   We had a poor past but now have a fabulous future

           b.   We will reign with our conquering Christ in His coming kingdom

III.   Conclusion

    A.   *We Ought to Start Practicing for Heaven's Choir*

    B.   *The Redeemer of Sinners Is Worthy of All Our Devotion*

    C.   *Heaven's Song Should Fill Our Hearts with Praise Every Day*

Heaven: The Praising Place

Series on Heaven   *Revelation 19:1–6*

I. **Introduction**
  A. *Heaven Will Be Well Populated (v. 1)*
    1. "I heard a great voice of much people"
    2. All the saints of ages past will be there
    3. All the resurrected and raptured will be there
  B. *The Gates of Hell Have Not Prevailed Against the Church*
    1. Millions have believed in spite of the cost
    2. Heaven will be a happy place of praising people
  C. *Why Will There Be All This Praise?*

II. **Body**
  A. *We Will Praise God for Who He Is (v. 1)*
    1. "Alleluia": He is worthy of our praise
    2. Salvation: He provides forgiveness and eternal life
      a. We were but sinners bound for hell
      b. His love reached us where we were
      c. His grace made our salvation possible
    3. Honor and glory: He lifts sinners from their shame
      a. He gives honor to the dishonorable
      b. He shares His glory with those who have none
      c. He makes fallen sinners citizens of heaven (Phil. 3:20)
    4. Power: His gospel contains power to save (Rom. 1:16)
  B. *We Will Praise God for What He Has Done (vv. 2–5)*
    1. "True and righteous are his judgments"
    2. God always does what is right
      a. "God always acts as becomes Him" (A. W. Tozer)
      b. The character of God assures us He always acts justly
    3. Here God has judged the corrupt tribulation religious system
      a. He has been putting down evil since the fall of man
      b. We should never question the righteous judgments of God

193

      4.   Saints in heaven praise God for His righteous acts

         a.   Angels join the chorus of praise for the righteousness of God

         b.   "Justice must always prevail . . . because the sovereign God will always prevail" (A. W. Tozer)

      5.   Jesus took our judgment on the Cross (Isa. 53:5–6)

  C. *We Will Praise God for What He Is Going to Do (v. 6)*

      1.   "The Lord God omnipotent reigneth"

         a.   Such is stated after a unanimous "alleluia"

         b.   All nature gets into this introduction

      2.   God will carry out His plan for the future

      3.   We can rest on God's promises for all our tomorrows

III. Conclusion

  A. *Is Your Heart Continually Filled with Praise?*

  B. *Are You on Your Way to Heaven, the Place of Perpetual Praise?*

  C. *Are You Praising God Daily in Preparation for the Praising Place?*

The Marriage of the Lamb

Series on Heaven   *Revelation 19:6–10*

I. **Introduction**
   A. *Here is History's Loudest Wedding Announcement (v. 6)*
      1. It is announced by the voice of a great multitude
      2. It is announced by the voice of many waters
      3. It is announced by the voice of mighty thunderings
   B. *The Wonderful Wedding Is Happening in Heaven*
      1. It is the marriage of Christ and His church
      2. It was prophesied by John the Baptist (John 3:25–30)
      3. It is described by Paul (Eph. 5:25–33)
         a. It compares earthly and Christ's marriage
         b. Christ's love for His bride is the ideal for all who marry
   C. *The Groom, the Bride, the Reception Supper Are Described*

II. **Body**
   A. *The Groom and His Gift Are Described (v. 7)*
      1. "The marriage of the Lamb is come"
         a. The marriage refers to the gift of eternal life through Christ's blood
         b. John the Baptist was the first to call Jesus the Lamb
         c. Old Testament sacrifices fulfilled in the death of Jesus
      2. Christ gave Himself for the church (Eph. 5:25)
      3. The Groom's marriage gift was purchased by His blood (1 Peter 1:19)
      4. It is the most valuable gift ever given by a groom to his bride
   B. *The Bride and Her Garments Are Described (vv. 7–8)*
      1. "His wife hath made herself ready"
         a. The bride is dressed for the wedding
         b. Her garments are gifts from the Groom
      2. The bride is dressed in fine linen, clean and white
         a. Her garments speak of the righteousness of the saints

195

b. We have no righteousness of our own (Isa. 64:6)

c. Our righteousness comes by faith (Rom. 10:4)

3. Righteous acts by believers are through the power of Christ (Eph. 2:10)

C. *The Reception Meal and the Guests Are Described (v. 9)*

1. "Blessed are they which are called [invited]"

2. Who are these invited guests?

a. John the Baptist identified himself as one of them (John 3:29)

b. The guests are the friends of the Bridegroom

3. Who are the friends of the Bridegroom?

a. They are saints who lived before the church age

b. Ancient heroes of the faith are coming to our wedding

4. What is the marriage supper of the Lamb?

a. Perhaps the greatest Communion service of all time

b. A celebration by those before and after the Cross

III. Conclusion

A. *Have You Responded to the Love of the Lamb?*

B. *Have You Trusted the Lamb as Your Savior, Your Lord?*

The King Is Coming

Revelation 19:11–21

I. Introduction
  A. *Here Is the Neglected Part of the Christmas Story*
   1. We rightly emphasize the prophecies and virgin birth (Isa. 7:14)
   2. We correctly focus on the stable in Bethlehem (Micah 5:2)
   3. We often neglect the King and His coming kingdom

  B. *A King Was Born in Bethlehem, Fulfilling the Scriptures*
   1. Mary's Son is to receive the throne of David (Luke 1:32)
   2. The wise men came seeking a newborn King (Matt. 2)

  C. *Redemption, the Rapture, the Revelation Is Contrasted*

II. Body
  A. *Here Is the Coming King (vv. 11–13)*
   1. "And I saw heaven opened"
   2. Christ departed heaven to enter Mary's womb
      a. This was to work the miracle of redemption (Phil. 2:5–8)
      b. He was born of a virgin in Bethlehem's stable (Luke 2)
      c. He died on the cross to redeem us (1 Peter 1:18–19)
   3. Christ is to depart heaven at the Rapture and return there with His bride (1 Thess. 4:13–18)
   4. Christ will depart from heaven riding a white horse
      a. This Rider is faithful and true (His sinless life)
      b. His clothing is/has been dipped in blood (His death on the cross)
      c. His name is called the Word of God (John 1:1–14)

  B. *Here Is the Commanding King (vv. 13–14)*
   1. "And the armies which were in heaven followed him"
   2. Now "Onward Christian Soldiers" takes on a new dimension

      a. These soldiers are clothed in fine white linen

      b. It is the clothing of the church at the marriage of the Lamb

      c. The church will become part of the army of heaven

  3. These soldiers follow their great Commander

      a. They ride white horses like their King

      b. We ought to follow our King every day in training for the future

  4. Christians should move from victory to victory not from defeat to defeat (v. 14)

C. *Here Is the Conquering King (vv. 15–21)*

  1. Our King will be armed with a sharp sword

      a. He conquers all by the power of His Word

      b. We can conquer daily by the same power

  2. Christ is the King of Kings and Lord of Lords (v. 16)

  3. Christ will end the Battle of Armageddon (vv. 17–21)

      a. Earth's armies will gather in the Middle East

      b. The world's military might will be arrayed against Christ at His coming

  4. The weapons of earth will be no match for our King

III. Conclusion

A. *Christians Are on Their Way to Ultimate Victory*

B. *Let's Expect Personal Victory Every Day*

C. *Satan Can Be Conquered by Those Who Belong to the Conqueror*

Heaven's Wonderful City

Series on Heaven Ends   *Revelation 21*

I. **Introduction**
  A. *Here Is the New Jerusalem*
    1. Here is John's vision of a city built in heaven
    2. The city that will come down to the new earth
      a. It descends, following the millennial reign of Christ
      b. It is the future capital city of the world
  B. *It Will Be a City Without Tears*
    1. All tears will be wiped away in this great city (v. 4)
    2. There will be no death, no sorrow, no crying, no pain
  C. *It Will Be a City of Wonders*

II. **Body**
  A. *First Is the Wonder of Its Size (vv. 10–17)*
    1. It will be surrounded by a great wall
      a. There will be twelve great gates in the wall
      b. Angels will be posted at each gate
      c. The names of the twelve tribes of Israel will be on the gates
    2. Twelve foundations are named for the twelve apostles
    3. The city will be fifteen hundred miles long, wide, and high
      a. It would stretch from Maine to Florida; from the Atlantic to Pike's Peak
      b. This is not all of heaven . . . just God's sample city
    4. There will be plenty of room for all the saved of the ages
  B. *Next Is the Wonder of Its Beauty (vv. 18–21)*
    1. The foundations will be garnished with precious stones
    2. The twelve gates will each be made of one pearl
    3. The streets of the city will be made of pure gold
  C. *Next Is the Wonder of Its Worship (v. 22)*

    1.   No temples will be needed in this great city
    2.   All worship will be directed to the One who is worthy
        a.   No false gods in this city—no idolatry, no heresy
        b.   The Lord God Almighty receives all the glory and praise
    3.   "Worthy Is the Lamb" is the praise chorus there

D. *Next Is the Wonder of Its Illumination (v. 23)*
    1.   There is no need of the sun or moon for light
    2.   Light comes from the glory of God
    3.   There will be no night there (v. 25)

E. *Next Is the Wonder of Its Inhabitants (vv. 24–27)*
    1.   Those saved by the blood of the Lamb
    2.   There will be no crime, no immorality, no violence
    3.   The citizens there are those whose names are in the Lamb's Book of Life

III. Conclusion

A. *Are You Ready for the City of Wonders?*
    1.   Have you placed your faith in Jesus?
    2.   Have you traded your darkness for His light?

B. *The Builder of Heaven's Wonderful City Is Waiting for You*

Christmas in Code

Luke 2:10

I. Introduction

A. *Christmas Is the Season of Wonders*
   1. It holds the wonder of the Virgin Birth (Isa. 7:14)
   2. It holds the wonder of the angels (to Mary, Joseph, and the shepherds)
   3. It holds the wonder of the Incarnation (Phil. 2:5–7)

B. *Christmas Was Observed in Times of Persecution*
   1. Here we talk freely of these wonders and ought to do so
   2. Persecution of Christians is increasing around the world
   3. Persecuted believers have sometimes had to code their beliefs

C. *A Coded Nursery Rhyme Was Composed for Christmas*

II. Body

A. *Mary Had a Little Lamb*
   1. "And she brought forth her firstborn son"
   2. Christmas didn't begin in Bethlehem
      a. God's promise to send His Son goes back to Eden (Gen. 3:15)
      b. Christmas was foreshadowed in Abel's first offering of a lamb
   3. John the Baptist would say, "Behold the Lamb of God" (John 1:29)
      a. No wonder shepherds were first at the manger and were the first evangelists
      b. Christians are headed for heaven, where the Lamb is worshiped
   4. The Lamb is the light in the holy city (Rev. 21:23)
   5. Those in heaven have their names in the Lamb's Book of Life (Rev. 21:27)

B. *His Fleece Was White as Snow*
   1. "And wrapped him in swaddling clothes"
   2. In the Bible, white is the color of holiness
      a. Sinners come to Christ to have their sins washed white (Isa. 1:18)

  b. Lost people are to be judged before the Great
      White Throne (Rev. 20:11)
  3. There are no racial implications in white being the
      color of holiness
      a. People of all colors are sinners (Rom. 3:23)
      b. People were all made of one blood (Acts
          17:26)
      c. People of all races are descendants of Adam
          . . . then of Noah
  4. The sinless One wrapped white (following the
      Cross) makes sinners clean
C. *Everywhere That Mary Went the Lamb Was Sure to Go*
  1. "And laid him in a manger"
  2. The manger speaks of the availability of Christ to
      all
      a. Jesus came to seek and save the lost (Luke
          19:10)
      b. He is able to save all who come to Him (Heb.
          7:25)
  3. Those who belong to Christ will never be alone
      a. "Lo, I am with you alway" (Matt. 28:18–20)
      b. "I will never leave thee nor forsake thee"
          (Heb. 13:5)
      c. All through life He is with us; then we go to be
          with Him (Ps. 23)

III. **Conclusion**
  A. *The Gospel Is So Simple It Can Be Coded in a Nursery
      Rhyme*
  B. *Childlike Faith in Christ Assures Us of Heaven*
  C. *Receive the Lamb and Enjoy His Fellowship Forever*

Still Time This Year

2 Corinthians 6:1–2; Acts 9:6; Revelation 22:12

I. **Introduction**
   A. *We Are in the Countdown of the Year*
      1. Only a few hours are left until the new year arrives
      2. All of life is a countdown, so every moment is important
   B. *Many Started This Year with Great Expectations*
      1. Some are disappointed in what they've accomplished
      2. Some think this has been a wasted year
   C. *Good News: There's Still Time to Make This Year Great*

II. **Body**
   A. *There Is Still Time to Be Saved (2 Cor. 6:1–2)*
      1. "Now is the day of salvation"
      2. You are alive and therefore have time to be saved
         a. You have time to admit you are a sinner (Luke 18:13; Rom. 3:23)
         b. You have time to believe God loves you (John 3:16)
         c. You have time to believe Christ died for you (Rom. 5:8)
         d. You have time to believe Christ arose (Rom. 10:9)
         e. You have time to call on Christ in faith to be saved (Rom. 10:13)
      3. Salvation takes place the moment we believe (Acts 16:31)
      4. Salvation is not complicated; all that is required is faith in Christ (Rom. 5:1)
      5. Those who trust Christ have assurance of salvation (1 John 5:11–13)
      6. One of the saddest Bible verses is a cry of those not saved in time (Jer. 8:20)
   B. *There Is Still Time to Surrender (Acts 9:6)*
      1. "What wilt thou have me to do?"
      2. The conversion of Saul is the story of a new beginning

a. Saul seemed to have everything but had nothing
b. Saul, a persecutor of Christians, was changed on the road to Damascus

3. Saul (Paul) trusted Christ and surrendered completely to Him
   a. This total surrender changed Paul's future and impacted the entire world
   b. Paul called for this kind of surrender for you and me (Rom. 12:1–2)

4. There is still time for you to stop resisting God's will for your life
   a. There is time to surrender old habits that hold you back
   b. There is time to surrender a temper that is destroying your marriage
   c. There is time to surrender to God's call to win souls, beginning today

C. *There Is Still Time for the Savior to Come (Rev. 22:12)*
   1. "And, behold, I come quickly"
   2. Christ, who died and rose again, will come again (John 14:1–3; 1 Thess. 4:13–18)
      a. He will come to raise the Christian dead
      b. He will come to catch away Christians to heaven
      c. He will come with rewards for those who have served Him
   3. Christ's coming will take place unexpectedly— maybe today (1 Cor. 15:51)

III. Conclusion

A. *Receive Christ Today and Be Sure of Heaven*
B. *Surrender to Christ Today and Make This Your Greatest Year*
C. *Seize This Moment for Christ While You've Time to Do So*

What Every Pastor Needs

A Charge to the Church   *Ephesians 4:11–12*
Following an Ordination

I. Introduction
   A. *Great Gifts Have Been Given to the Church*
      1. The church has received the foundational work of apostles and prophets
      2. It has received evangelists, pastors, and teachers in local ministries
   B. *Pastors Are Key to Local Church Health and Development*
      1. Great potential rests in a strong pastor-congregation bond
      2. Pastors and their people can shake communities for Christ
   C. *What Does a Pastor Need to Be Effective?*

II. Body
   A. *A Pastor Needs a Church That Understands the Work of a Pastor (2 Cor. 2:16)*
      1. Some think pastors have an easy life, working only a few days a week
      2. Few understand the pressures of the ministry
         a. It carries the burden of souls in the balance
         b. It has the difficulty of keeping unity in a church
         c. It experiences the extreme fatigue that follows preaching
         d. It is aware of the lack of time to do what needs to be done
      3. Paul: "Who is sufficient for these things?'"
      4. Pastors need understanding people who love them
         a. They need people who are loyal and defend them against gossip
         b. They need people who encourage them when others criticize
         c. They need people who are peacemakers within the congregation

   B. *A Church That Prays Is Bigger than the Pastor (Acts 1:14)*
- 1. Long hours facing difficulties can drain a pastor's strength, dull his vision
  - a. A pastor may become problem conscious instead of power conscious
  - b. A pastor may become so weary his prayer life suffers
  - c. A pastor may become discouraged by listening to the downers
- 2. Consider those praying people in the Upper Room
  - a. Both men and women were gathered for prayer
  - b. They "continued" in prayer; it was not a short meeting
  - c. Pentecost proved the effectiveness of their prayers (Acts 2)
- 3. Paul asked for the prayers of others: "Brethren, pray for us" (2 Thess. 3:1)
- 4. Hundreds met to pray before Spurgeon preached; the same for J. Wilbur Chapman

   C. *A Witnessing Church Wins More Souls than the Pastor (Acts 8:4)*
- 1. The early church experienced dynamic growth because all became witnesses
  - a. Deacon Philip did personal evangelism (Acts 8:26–38)
  - b. "They . . . went everywhere preaching the word" (Acts 8:4)
- 2. Happy is the pastor whose people continually win souls
  - a. It demonstrates he has taught his people well and set the example
  - b. He has perfected his church to do the work of the ministry
  - c. He has done the work of an evangelist, made full proof of his ministry (2 Tim. 4:5)

III. Conclusion

   A. *Are You the Pastor's Critic or His Encourager?*

   B. *How Big Are Your Prayers for Your Pastor and Church?*

   C. *Are You the Soul Winner Your Pastor Needs You to Be?*

Honor Your Pastor

Sermon for Installing a New Pastor   *1 Timothy 5:17–18*

I. Introduction
    A. *A Church and Its Pastor Is an Exciting Combination*
        1. Officers of the church are ordained by the Lord
        2. There is power in a congregation and its leaders
            a. They transform people and communities
            b. They change lives and the world by the power of the gospel
    B. *The Pastor Is an Important Part of This Divine Plan*
        1. A God-ordained preacher of the Word holds a unique position
        2. He is the one who feeds the flock of God and leads them in outreach
    C. *How Shall We Honor This Man and His Office?*

II. Body
    A. *Honor Your Pastor by Praying for Him*
        1. Why does your pastor need prayer?
            a. He is fighting supernatural enemies (Eph. 6)
            b. He is human and susceptible to temptation (1 Cor. 10:13)
            c. He needs wisdom for counseling, leading, preaching (James 1:5)
        2. Pray for your pastor every day for strength, wisdom, discernment, and power
    B. *Honor Your Pastor by Praising Him*
        1. Pastors need encouraging; the enemy tries to discourage them
        2. Good words lift and revitalize; give some to your pastor often (Prov. 12:25)
        3. Focus on your pastor's strong points and speak of them often (Phil 4:8)
    C. *Honor Your Pastor by Protecting Him*
        1. Your pastor will be under attack
            a. He will be under attack by the powers of darkness
            b. He will be under attack by those whom no one can please

        c.   He will be under attack by those who are easily offended

    2.   Protect your pastor by putting out fires in the congregation

    3.   Protect your pastor by refusing to pass along gossip

  D. *Honor Your Pastor by Partnering with Him*

    1.   The ministry can be lonely work

        a.   People often promise more than they deliver

        b.   Most church work is done by a faithful few

        c.   Make sure you are part of this valuable minority

    2.   Volunteer to help in the work of the ministry: teaching, visiting, soul winning

        a.   You and the entire church will benefit from this kind of involvement

        b.   Your pastor will be encouraged when he witnesses your willingness to work

  E. *Honor Your Pastor by Paying Him*

    1.   Pay "double honor" for those who labor in the Word and doctrine

    2.   "The laborer is worthy of his reward"

    3.   Lift your pastor's burden of financial stress by paying him well

III. Conclusion

  A. *Honoring Your Pastor Will Bless His Family*

  B. *Honoring Your Pastor Will Bless the Church*

  C. *Honoring Your Pastor Will Bring Eternal Rewards*

The Preacher Who Couldn't Quit

Jeremiah 20:9

I. **Introduction**
  A. *Jeremiah Was the Weeping Prophet*
     1. Jeremiah lived in a troubled time
     2. He was given a difficult message to proclaim
     3. The trials of his people made Jeremiah a man of tears
  B. *Speaking Out for God Brought Jeremiah Persecution*
     1. Telling the truth cost this prophet his freedom
     2. He was stricken by Pashur, the son of the high priest
     3. Finding himself in prison, Jeremiah wanted to resign
  C. *Why Couldn't This Discouraged Preacher Quit?*

II. **Body**
  A. *He Was Sure of God's Call*
     1. "I will not speak anymore in his name"
        a. Jeremiah had been telling people about God
        b. He had been speaking with God's authority
     2. Serving God had been his life's work (1:4)
     3. At first, Jeremiah had been afraid to preach (1:5–6)
     4. God confirmed Jeremiah's call to the ministry (1:7–9)
        a. "Thou shalt go to all that I shall send thee"
        b. "I have put my words in thy mouth"
     5. How could Jeremiah quit when he had been called by God?
  B. *He Was Saturated with God's Word*
     1. "His word was in my heart as a burning fire"
        a. Preaching was more than an occupation to Jeremiah
        b. His passion in life was to give God's message to his people
     2. Jeremiah had filled his mind with God's Word
        a. This kept him mindful of God's love for people in spite of their sins

209

        b.   He had witnessed the power of God to change lives

    3.   Years of preaching now prevented Jeremiah from quitting

        a.   It was like trying to quench a roaring fire

        b.   Jeremiah was a preacher with fire in his bones

    4.   The Scriptures kept reminding Jeremiah of his calling

        a.   He must tell the people of the seriousness of sin

        b.   He must tell the people of God's forgiveness being available

C. *He Was Sure His Message Would Meet the Needs of His People*

    1.   Jeremiah's confidence in God's Word brought a conflict to his mind

        a.   He knew God's message would irritate some

        b.   He knew the people needed to hear in spite of their opposition

    2.   Holding back placed Jeremiah in great distress

        a.   He became weary with his struggle for silence

        b.   He finally gave up and went back to preaching

III. Conclusion

A. *Have You Become Weary in Your Service for God?*

B. *Don't Quit! People Need to Hear What You Have to Say*

A Preacher's Priorities

2 Timothy 4:1–8

I. Introduction

A. *Make Full Proof of Your Ministry*

    1. Timothy was charged by a man who practiced what he preached

    2. Paul made the most of his time and talents

B. *There Is a Danger of Being Overwhelmed by the Ministry*

    1. The care of souls, teaching, counseling, discipling can become overwhelming

    2. Visitation, evangelism, studying, administrating, preaching can become overwhelming

    3. "Who is sufficient for these things?" (2 Cor. 2:16)

C. *What Priorities Are Demanded in a Preacher's Life?*

II. Body

A. *People Must Have Priority over Programs (Matt. 20:28)*

    1. The ministry is a people-centered calling

    2. Jesus set the example

        a. He came to serve, not to be served

        b. He was always reaching out to troubled people

    3. This is a program-centered time in church history

        a. So many tested schemes are available to reach people

        b. Growth through gimmickry beckons ministers today

    4. Service without love for people is just putting in time (1 Cor. 13)

        a. All preaching, teaching, and advising are just noise without love

        b. Love centers on the needs of people, not fine-tuning programs

B. *Preaching Must Have Priority over Politics (2 Tim. 4:2)*

    1. "Preach the word" is a clear call to the primacy of gospel preaching

    a. No earthly approach to problems compares to the gospel

    b. The gospel contains the power of God, not so any other message (Rom. 1:16)

2. The temptation is to get involved in political approaches to problems

    a. This often caters to pride in the preacher because of public attention

    b. The press is impressed by a preacher leading a political charge

    c. We must not choose temporal solutions over eternal ones

3. Preaching the Word requires studying the Word (2 Tim. 2:15)

4. Preaching the Word requires faith in the power of the Word to change lives

5. Preaching the Word builds churches that produce mature Christians

C. *Prayer Must Have Priority over Promotion (Acts 4:31–33)*

1. The early church prayed and spoke the Word with boldness

    a. Their powerful praying and preaching shook the world

    b. Communities need churches that pray with power

2. Promotion demonstrates what modern methods can do

3. Prayer demonstrates what God can do

4. A praying pastor will produce a praying church

    a. Church board meetings will be called for nothing but prayer

    b. Special congregational meetings will be called just to pray

III. Conclusion

A. *A Pastor Making Full Proof of His Ministry Has a Mighty Impact*

B. *Pastors Who Keep Their Priorities Right Will Finish Well (vv. 6–8)*

Dual Citizenship

Philippians 3:20; Romans 13:1–8;
Acts 4:19–20; 5:29

I. Introduction
A. *All Christians Have Dual Citizenship*
1. We are citizens of heaven, traveling through this earth
2. We are citizens of this earth on our way to heaven
B. *This Dual Citizenship Raises Three Questions*
1. What are our responsibilities as citizens of heaven?
2. What are our responsibilities as citizens of earth?
3. What do we do when these responsibilities clash?

II. Body
A. *What Are Our Responsibilities as Citizens of Heaven?*
(Phil. 3:20)
1. How did we become citizens of heaven?
    a. We were born citizens of earth by natural birth
    b. We were born into heavenly citizenship through faith (1 Peter 1:3)
2. We are to represent our King while on this earth
    a. Through faith in Jesus, Paul became a new man (2 Cor. 5:17)
    b. He then became an ambassador for Christ in this world (2 Cor. 5:20)
    c. In this role, he called others to be reconciled to God
3. We are to live on earth in a manner that causes others to glorify our King
    a. "Let your light so shine before men" (Matt. 5:16)
    b. We are to live blamelessly in order to be lights in a dark world (Phil. 2:15–16)
4. The citizens of heaven should be easily identified on earth because of how they live
B. *What Are Our Responsibilities as Citizens of Earth?*
(Rom. 13:1–8)
1. Citizens of heaven should be model citizens of earth

    2. We are to be subject to leaders of the land
        a. We must recognize that government is ordained by God
        b. We must honor those who enforce the law and keep the peace
    3. We are to pay our taxes (v. 6)
    4. We are to show respect to leaders (v. 7)
    5. We are also to pray for those who have authority over us (1 Tim. 2:1–3)
        a. "Supplications, prayers, intercessions, giving of thanks for leaders"
        b. Our prayers for authorities can contribute to a peaceful life

C. *What Do We Do When These Responsibilities Clash? (Acts 4:19–20; 5:29)*
    1. Earthly authorities sometimes oppose the work of God. What then?
    2. The lame man at the temple was healed (Acts 3:1–8)
        a. The man who had been lame was now leaping and praising God
        b. This miracle provided opportunities to preach the gospel
    3. Angry leaders demanded Peter and John stop preaching
    4. These disciples had been commissioned to tell people of God's love
        a. They explained they were responsible to tell what they knew
        b. They said they must obey God rather than men (5:29)

III. Conclusion

A. *How Are You Representing Jesus as a Citizen of Heaven?*

B. *Are You Recognized as a Good Citizen of Earth?*

C. *Are You Committed to Obeying God Whatever the Cost?*

Three Constants in an Age of Change

Isaiah 59:1–2

I. **Introduction**
  A. *We Live in a Changing World*
    1. Each generation witnesses changes that would astound their ancestors
    2. Scientific and technological breakthroughs have changed lifestyles
    3. Even weather patterns and common locations of natural disasters change
  B. *Three Things Are Constants; They Remain the Same*
    1. God's power to save remains the same
    2. God's ability to hear and answer prayer remains the same
    3. The destructiveness of sin remains the same
  C. *Let Us Explore These Unchanging Truths*

II. **Body**
  A. *God's Power to Save Remains the Same*
    1. "Behold, the LORD's hand is not shortened that it cannot save"
      a. This is a statement that has remained true through the ages
      b. It is a statement that will remain true forever
    2. God is able to save from physical danger
      a. He opened the Red Sea to save Israel from Pharaoh's army
      b. He delivered Daniel from death in the lion's den
    3. God is able to save the soul from death
      a. He saved religious Nicodemus from dead legalism (John 3:3–5, 16)
      b. He saved the thief on the cross and guaranteed him paradise (Luke 23:39–43)
  B. *God's Ability to Hear and Answer Prayer Remains the Same*
    1. "Neither his ear heavy, that it cannot hear"
    2. God heard the prayers of His people while they were slaves in Egypt (Exod. 3:7–8)

        a.   He called Moses to deliver them and tell them He had heard their prayers

        b.   He promised to bring them into a good land flowing with milk and honey

   3.   God has given great promises of answered prayer throughout the Bible

        a.   He invited to Jeremiah to pray big and expect answers (Jer. 33:3)

        b.   Jesus invited believers to ask and receive (Matt. 7:7–8)

   4.   The early church prayed and thousands came to Christ (Acts 1:14; 4:31–33)

   5.   George Müeller prayed and hundreds of orphans were fed and clothed

   6.   Christians prove God answers prayer every day in their personal lives

   7.   Churches pray and demonstrate God's promises of answered prayer are true

C.   *The Destructiveness of Sin Remains the Same*

   1.   "Your iniquities have separated between you and your God"

   2.   Sin in our lives keeps our prayers from being answered

        a.   "If I regard iniquity in my heart, the Lord will not hear me" (Ps. 66:18)

        b.   Elijah prayed with great power because of the way he lived (James 5:17–18)

   3.   The progression of sin is lust, sin, death (James 1:15)

   4.   We cannot escape the consequences of sin (Num. 32:23)

III. Conclusion

A.   *Our Need for Salvation Remains the Same*

B.   *The Love of God for Sinners Remains the Same*

C.   *The Way of Salvation Remains the Same*

What Makes God Wonder?

Isaiah 59:16

I. Introduction
A. *Many Things Make Us Wonder*
1. We behold the seven wonders of the world
2. We wonder at sights and sounds that go beyond our understanding
3. We wonder at a newborn baby, a raging storm, a volcano erupting, an earthquake

B. *We Wonder at the Great Works of God (Ps. 77:11–14)*
1. We behold the wonders of His great creation
2. We behold the wonders of His great love: the Incarnation, the Cross, the Resurrection
3. We behold the great wonders of fulfilled prophecy: the prospect of Christ's return

C. *What Makes God Wonder?*

II. Body
A. *God Must Wonder at the Passiveness of His People over Sin (vv. 2–14)*
1. Consider the terrible moral and spiritual conditions in Isaiah's time
   a. It was a time of violence and dishonesty (vv. 2–3)
   b. It was a time of injustice and crooked dealings (v. 4)
   c. It was a time when evil seemed to be triumphing over good (vv. 5–8)
2. Does any of this seem familiar? Do you see evil on the rise today?
3. Confusion reigned among the people
   a. "We roar all like bears, and mourn sour like doves" (v. 11)
   b. No strong public outcry against these sins could be heard
4. "The sins of a nation bring public judgment when not restrained" (Matthew Henry)

B. *God Must Wonder at the Persecution of His People Who Stand for the Truth*

217

1. "He that departeth from evil maketh himself a prey" (v. 15)
   a. Those who stand against evil often place themselves in jeopardy
   b. Consider the persecutions of the prophets in the past
2. Jesus is the prime example of one who suffered for righteousness
   a. His pure life turned the legalists of His day against Him
   b. Those who claimed to be righteous crucified the righteous One
3. Paul said this is an ever-enduring condition
   a. "All that will live godly in Christ Jesus shall suffer persecution" (2 Tim. 3:12)
   b. Paul had suffered for serving his Lord (2 Cor. 11:23–30)

C. *God Must Wonder at the Prayerlessness of His People in Sinful Situations*
   1. "He saw that there was no man and wondered that there was no intercessor"
   2. Interceding for those in desperate situations has been a mark of heroes of the faith
      a. Abraham interceded for Lot and those in sinful Sodom (Gen. 18:21–25)
      b. Moses interceded for Israel when they deserved judgment (Exod. 32:30–35)
      c. Jeremiah interceded with tears over the sins of his people (Jer. 14)
   3. Jesus interceded for those who were crucifying Him (Luke 23:34)
   4. The early church interceded for Peter when he was in prison (Acts 12)
   5. We ought to follow their examples and pray fervently for all church leaders

III. Conclusion

A. *Where Are Those Who Will Speak Out Against Sin?*
B. *Where Are Those Who Will Stand for Truth in Spite of the Cost?*
C. *Where Are the Intercessors We Need in This Crucial Hour?*

How Big Is God?

Isaiah 41:10; Matthew 17:20;
Philippians 4:19; Psalm 18:3

I. **Introduction**
   A. *We All Face Problems Bigger than Ourselves*
      1. We all go through things we didn't think we would
      2. Some go through things they didn't think they could
   B. *Where Do We Turn When We're Out of Our League?*
      1. How do we cope with fears beyond our courage to fight?
      2. How do we tap God's power when our faith is small?
      3. How do we pay bills that are greater than our income and savings?
      4. How do we conquer enemies who are too strong for us?
   C. *Enter God Almighty*

II. **Body**
   A. *God Is Bigger than Our Fears (Isa. 41:10)*
      1. "Fear thou not; for I am with thee"
      2. Fear is common to all
         a. Fear was the first evidence of the Fall (Gen. 3:10)
         b. God was here before fear came on the scene (Gen. 1:1)
         c. God will be here when all the fears of the ages have departed (Rev. 21:6)
      3. God guarantees He is greater than all our fears (for I am with thee)
         a. Consider all the "fear nots" in the Bible
         b. Remember people of faith who conquered their fears: Moses, Joshua, David, etc.
      4. The resurrection of Christ declares He has overcome our greatest fear
   B. *God Is Better than Our Faith (Matt. 17:20)*
      1. "If you have faith as a grain of mustard seed"

219

2. It is not the size of our faith but the strength of our Lord that makes the difference
   a. Mountain-moving faith rests in our omnipotent God
   b. Meek Moses lifted his rod and God parted the Red Sea
3. Fearful, grieving Martha saw Lazarus rise at Christ's call (John 11:43–44)

C. *God Is Richer than Our Debts (Phil 4:19)*
   1. "My God shall supply all your need"
      a. He owns the cattle on a thousand hills (Ps. 50:10)
      b. Our rich heavenly Father has no shortage of funds
   2. No creditor has anything on his ledger beyond what God can provide
   3. Sometimes in giving we tap God's boundless supply (Luke 6:38)

D. *God Is Stronger than Our Enemies (Ps. 18:3)*
   1. "So shall I be saved from mine enemies"
   2. How did the psalmist plan to find safety from his enemies?
      a. He said he would find safety by calling on the Lord
      b. "The clefts of the rock are safe hiding places" (C. H. Spurgeon)
   3. Christians have the armor of God to protect them from all their foes (Eph. 6:11–18)

III. Conclusion
   A. *The Believer's Victory Is Assured in the Gospel*
      1. Since Christ died and rose again, He achieved the ultimate victory
      2. The One who saved us is able to keep us all the way to heaven
   B. *God Is Big Enough to Meet All the Needs of Those Who Trust Him*

Scripture Index